i before e
(except after c)

The true art of memory is the art of attention.

SAMUEL JOHNSON

i before e
(except after c)

old-school ways
to remember stuff

JUDY PARKINSON

Illustrations by LOUISE MORGAN

MICHAEL O'MARA BOOKS LIMITED

First published in Great Britain in 2007 by
Michael O'Mara Books Limited
9 Lion Yard, Tremadoc Road
London SW4 7NQ

A CIP catalogue record for this book is available
from the British Library

Papers used by Michael O'Mara Books Limited are natural,
recyclable products made from wood grown in sustainable
forests. The manufacturing processes conform to the
environmental regulations of the country of origin.

ISBN 978-1-84317-249-9

11 13 15 17 19 20 18 16 14 12

www.mombooks.com

Cover design by Angie Allison

Front-cover title lettering by Toby Buchan

Extra illustration on page 82 © David Woodroffe

Designed and typeset by Martin Bristow

Printed and bound in Great Britain by Clays Ltd, St Ives plc

Contents

Introduction

═══

'Thirty days hath September, April, June and November . . .' How many times, perhaps anxiously awaiting payday, have you muttered this saying to yourself? Or racked your brains for the name of the king who succeeded Henry II, in order to squash that bumptious, know-all guest at a dinner party?

No doubt about it, memory's a funny business. But in a happier and perhaps less hectic age, many useful, if not invaluable facts were taught by the use of mnemonics, simple memory aids which, once learned, fixed the information in the brain for ever. This book takes a nostalgic look back at the many quirky and amusing ways you were taught to remember 'stuff' at school or university, and which can still be used to solve a problem or cap an argument. Packed with clever verses, engaging acronyms, curious – and sometimes hilarious – sayings, *i before e (except after c)* includes all the mnemonics you could ever need (and some you probably won't).

From simple rhymes about spelling – 'S is the verb and C is the noun,/That's the rule that runs the town' will sort out 'practise/practice', 'license/licence', and so on for you – to useful phrases for recalling important facts from history – 'divorced, beheaded, died,/divorced, beheaded, survived' gives, in chronological order, the fates of Henry VIII's six wives – life-saving acronyms such as 'ABC' (Airways, Breathing, Circulation), or just useful bits of general knowledge – 'There's a little RED PORT LEFT in the bottle' tells you the colour, name and position of navigation lights on a ship or aircraft – *i before e* is an amusing collection of the many ingenious mind tricks devised to help us learn and understand.

1
The English Language

The Alphabet

Before we could read the complete works of Shakespeare, as children we first had to learn the alphabet. Some of us will have recited the letters to the tune of 'Twinkle, Twinkle, Little Star', a method made famous by Big Bird from the TV programme *Sesame Street*.

The song was first copyrighted in 1835 by Charles Bradlee, a Boston music publisher, who called it: 'The ABC, a German air with variations for the flute with an easy accompaniment for the pianoforte.'

> *a–b–c–d–e–f–g,*
> *h–i–j–k–l–m–n–o–p,*
> *q–r–s–t–u–v,*
> *w–x–y and z.*
> *Now I know my A, B, Cs,*
> *next time won't you sing with me?*

Because the letters l–m–n–o–p have to be sung twice as fast as the rest of the letters in the rhyme, some children have mistakenly assumed that 'elemenopee' is a word. For the rhyme to work with the Z, you have to use the American pronunciation of 'zee' rather than 'zed'.

If you didn't sing the ABC to the tune of 'Twinkle, Twinkle, Little Star' then you might have used the tune of 'Baa, Baa, Black Sheep' instead, which has a very similar rhythm and melody.

The following ABC memory rhyme entitled 'The Tragical Death of A, Apple Pie, Who Was Cut in Pieces, and Eaten By Twenty-Six Gentlemen, With Whom All Little People Ought to be Very Well Acquainted', was a popular way of teaching the alphabet to youngsters in the nineteenth century, though it dates back at least as far as the reign of Charles II (1660–85).

A was an apple pie
B bit it,
C cut it,
D dealt it,
E eats it,
F fought for it,
G got it,
H had it,
I inspected it,
J jumped for it,
K kept it,
L longed for it,
M mourned for it,
N nodded at it,
O opened it,
P peeped in it,
Q quartered it,
R ran for it,
S stole it,
T took it,
U upset it,
V viewed it,
W wanted it,
X, **Y** and **Z** all wished for
and had a piece in hand.

The Five Vowels

The English alphabet has five soft vowels: A E I O U. This sequence of letters generally tends to roll off the tongue quite naturally, but for anyone who has trouble remembering the order of vowels, here are a couple of useful phrases:

Ann's **E**gg **I**s **O**n **U**s

Anthony's **E**go **I**s **O**ver **U**sed

Parts of Speech

After learning the alphabet, the next step is to come up with coherent sentences. The rhyme below categorizes each of the parts of speech, giving a clear example of the different type of word. It dates back to 1855 and was written by David B. Tower and Benjamin F. Tweed:

Three little words you often see
Are **articles**: *a, an* and *the.*

A **noun**'s the name of any thing,
As: *school* or *garden, toy* or *swing.*

Adjectives tell the kind of noun,
As: *great, small, pretty, white* or *brown.*

Verbs tell of something being done:
To read, write, count, sing, jump or *run.*

How things are done, the **adverbs** tell,
As: *slowly, quickly, badly, well.*

Conjunctions join the words together,
As: men *and* women, wind *or* weather.

The **preposition** stands before
A noun as: *in* or *through* a door.

The **interjection** shows surprise
As: 'Oh, how pretty!' or 'Ah! How wise!'

The whole are called the parts of speech,
Which reading, writing, speaking teach.

A different rhyme called 'The Parts of Speech' is similarly pithy, and serves as another useful reminder of the different components of the English language. The origin of these verses is unknown.

Every name is called a **noun**,
As *field* and *fountain, street* and *town.*

In place of noun the **pronoun** stands,
As *he* and *she* can clap their hands.

The **adjective** describes a thing,
As *magic* wand and *bridal* ring.

The **verb** means action, something done –
To *read*, to *write*, to *jump*, to *run*.

How things are done, the **adverbs** tell,
As *quickly, slowly, badly, well*.

The **preposition** shows relation,
As *in* the street, or *at* the station.

Conjunctions join, in many ways,
Sentences, words, *or* phrase *and* phrase.

The **interjection** cries out, 'Hark!
I need an exclamation mark!'

Through poetry, we learn how each
Of these make up the **Parts of Speech**.

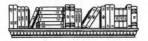

What's a Preposition?

After the alphabet and parts of speech come more technicalities. Any word that fits in the space of this sentence is a preposition: The squirrel ran — the tree.

For example, over, under, after, around, through, up, on, to, from, by, etc. Other prepositions include: in, at, for, between, among, of.

What's a Conjunction?

Conjunctions are words used to join two independent clauses. Most of us are careless with punctuation, especially now when we often use shortcuts in emails and text messages. But this FAN BOYS mnemonic helps if you want to remember the co-ordinating conjunctions, of which the most important are 'and', 'or' and 'but':

FAN BOYS

For, **A**nd, **N**or, **B**ut, **O**r, **Y**et, **S**o

Rules of Punctuation

Cecil Hartley's poem from *Principles of Punctuation* (1818) reveals the old-fashioned way that people were advised how to interpret punctuation when reading sentences out loud.

The stops point out, with truth, the time of pause
A sentence doth require at ev'ry clause.
At ev'ry comma, stop while *one* you count;
At semicolon, *two* is the amount;
A colon doth require the time of *three*;
The period *four*, as learned men agree.

Though it's not a verse that most grammarians would encourage these days, it does give an idea of the difference between each type of punctuation mark.

A Verse on Commas

A cat has claws at the ends of its paws.
A comma's a pause at the end of a clause.

On Colons

H. W. Fowler conjures up a useful visual image of the job done by the colon, which he says 'delivers the goods that have been invoiced in the preceding words'.

A Verse on the Exclamation Mark

The following seventeenth-century rhyme appeared in *Treatise of Stops, Points, or Pauses, and of Notes which are used in Writing and Print* (1680):

This stop denotes our Suddain Admiration,
Of what we Read, or Write, or giv Relation,
And is always cal'd an Exclamation.

> The art of punctuation is of infinite consequence in writing; as it contributes to the perspicuity, and consequently to the beauty of every composition.
>
> JOSEPH ROBERTSON

Writing Stories

And when you put all these elements together to write your first novel, don't forget the main elements of storytelling:

Viewpoint
Mood
Plot
Characters
Theme
Setting

If the VMPCTS acronym doesn't trip easily off the tongue, this phrase should help to keep it firmly in mind:

Very **M**any **P**upils **C**ome **T**o **S**chool

Learning Lines

How do actors memorize scripts? Learning lines by repetition is the most obvious way, but many actors also refer to the beat of the script, that is, the rhythm of the words, which they literally tune into. Some plays are easier to learn than others. Shakespeare's texts are highly memorable because they are fun and fruity; full of puns (often extremely bawdy ones), rhymes and alliterations:

Whereat, with blade, with bloody blameful blade,
He bravely breach'd his boiling bloody breast.

Another mnemonic secret of the English poetic tradition
is the rhythm of the iambic pentameter. An iamb is a beat
with one soft syllable and one strong syllable, and a series

of five iambs forms the heartbeat of English poetry: its familiarity makes it easy to remember, especially in the works of Shakespeare.

From *Hamlet*:

To be / or not / to be / that is / the question.

From the Sonnets:

Shall I / compare / thee to / a sum/mer's day?
Thou art / more love/ly and / more tem/perate:
Rough winds / do shake / the dar/ling buds / of May,
And sum/mer's lease / hath all / too short / a date.

Setting a text to a well-known tune and rhythm is a useful method of memorizing the words. Why not try singing Homer's *Odyssey*, Coleridge's 'The Rime of the Ancient Mariner' or one of Shakespeare's sonnets to the tune of your favourite nursery rhyme or pop song? You can remember the words using a combination of rhymes, rhythms and repetition.

2
To Spell or Not to Spell

Everyone has a different level of ability when it comes to spelling. Some of us are lucky enough to be able to spell 'supercalifragilisticexpialidocious' without a second thought, while others are stumped by the simplest word. For those who fall into the latter category, perhaps they weren't taught the right sort of spelling mnemonics . . .

I before E (except after C)

This phrase is drummed into children at primary school and it works in the sentence: 'Receive a Piece of Pie.' But all rules invariably have exceptions, just to make life difficult:

> *i* before *e*, except after *c*
> or when sounded like *a*
> as in *neighbour* and *weigh*

A similar version ends with the line: 'as in *weigh, neigh* or *sleigh*'. Numerous exceptions to the rule include the words *neither, height, leisure* and *weird*.

A rhyme with an extended rule used more commonly in British schools clarifies things a little further:

> When the sound is *ee*
> It's *i* before *e* except after *c*

However, even the extended rule has a number of exceptions: words such as *caffeine, protein* and *seize* are *e* before *i* despite having a long *ee* sound. Also, the plurals of *–cy* words end with *–cies*, which is another exception to the *i* before *e* rule, as are *science*-related words.

Hence, yet another addendum has had to be applied to the original saying:

> *i* before *e*, except after *c*
> or when sounded like *a*
> as in *neighbour* and *weigh*;
> drop this rule when *-c* sounds as *-sh*

Thus words such as *ancient, efficient* and *species* become covered by the additional rule.

The Vagaries of English Spelling

The English language is full of complexities and contradictions, which can make the spelling and pronunciation of certain words quite difficult to predict. Here is an anonymous poem that cleverly highlights a number of problem words that all learners of English, young and old, should watch out for in particular.

> I take it you already know
> Of *tough* and *bough* and *cough* and *dough*?
> Others may stumble, but not you,
> On *hiccough, thorough, lough* and *through*?
> Well done! And now you wish, perhaps,
> To learn of less familiar traps?
> Beware of *heard*, a dreadful word
> That looks like *beard* and sounds like *bird*,
> And *dead*: it's said like *bed*, not *bead* –
> For goodness' sake, don't call it *deed*!
> Watch out for *meat* and *great* and *threat*
> (They rhyme with *suite* and *straight* and *debt*).
> A *moth* is not a moth in *mother*,
> Nor *both* in *bother*, *broth* in *brother*,
> And *here* is not a match for *there*,
> Nor *dear* and *fear* for *bear* and *pear*.
> And then there's *dose* and *rose* and *lose* –
> Just look them up – and *goose* and *choose*,
> And *cork* and *work*, and *card* and *ward*,
> And *font* and *front*, and *word* and *sword*,
> And *do* and *go*, and *thwart* and *cart* –
> Come, come, I've hardly made a start!
> A dreadful language? Man alive!
> I'd mastered it when I was five!

License or Licence?
Practise or Practice?

A handy way to remember when to use an 's' and when to use a 'c' is illustrated perfectly in this pithy rhyme:

> S is the verb and C is the noun,
> That's the rule that runs the town.

The DVLA is licensed to issue driving licences.
A doctor practises medicine at his practice.

Affect or Effect?

The RAVEN mnemonic is useful when working out whether to use 'affect' or 'effect' in a sentence:

Remember: **A**ffect, **V**erb; **E**ffect, **N**oun

The woman was affected by the effect of the film.

Reading with care will secure everybody from false spelling; for books are always well spelled.

PHILIP STANHOPE,
4TH EARL OF CHESTERFIELD

Spelling Aids: A Useful Selection

The spellings of some words appear to have no logic whatsoever, and the only way not to look like a dunce is to recite a well-worn mnemonic phrase to help you to remember, or even to invent one of your own.

———

ACCELERATOR

A Cruel **C**reature – imagine words and pictures
to remind you to write two Cs.

———

ACCESSIBLE

-able or -ible?
Say out loud, '**I** am always access**i**ble.'

———

ACCIDENTALLY

Two Cs and an ally. Make up a story:
two cats accidentally scratched your friend and ally.

———

ACCOMMODATION

Again two Cs and two Ms,
and don't forget that second O after the second M.

Comfortable **C**hairs, **O**r **M**odern **M**ats, **O**r . . . ?

ADDRESS

Directly **D**elivered letters are **S**afe and **S**ound.

AEROPLANE

All **E**ngines **R**unning **O**kay.

ALMOND

ALmonds are ovALs.

ARGUMENT

A Rude **G**irl **U**ndresses – **M**y **E**yes **N**eed **T**aping.

Another way to check your spelling is to find short words within. Think of chewing GUM when you chew over an arGUMent.

ARITHMETIC

A Rat **I**n **T**he **H**ouse **M**ay **E**at **T**he **I**ce Cream.

ASSASSINATION

This word is made up of four short words:

ASS ASS I NATION

ASTHMA

The cause of AsthmA –
Sensitivity To Household Mites.

AUTUMN

There's an N at the end of Autumn. Think of N standing
for November, when it's the end of Autumn and beginning
of winter.

BARE or BEAR

Imagine scenarios relating to the two words.

It's bathtime with a BAR of soap on your BARE skin.

A BEAR is scary and fills you with FEAR.

BEAUTIFUL

Big Elephants Are Usually BEAUtiful.

BECAUSE

Big Elephants Can Always Understand
Small Elephants.

Big Elephants Can't Always
Use Small Exits.

BELIEVE

This word obeys the *i* before *e* rule, and there's also a perfect word association within.

Do you beLIEve a LIE?

BISCUIT

Some believe this word is derived from two French words – *bis cuit* meaning 'twice cooked'. The easy way to remember how to spell it is with this phrase:

BIScuits are **C**rumbled **U**p **I**nto **T**iny pieces.

BROCCOLI

We know it's good for us, but it's tricky to spell. Remember that broccoli would never **C**ause **COLI**c.

CAPITAL or CAPITOL

The capitAl city of Greece is Athens.
PAris is the capitAl of FrAnce.

Most capitOl buildings have dOmes.
There's a capitOl in WashingtOn.

CHAOS

Cyclones, **H**urricanes **A**nd **O**ther **S**torms create chaos.

CHARACTER

CHARlie's **ACT** is **ER**otic.

COMMITTEE

Remember: **M**any **M**eetings **T**ake **T**ime –
Everyone's **E**xhausted!

CONSCIENCE

It's not pronounced how it's spelt.
It's SCIENCE with CON at the beginning.

CORRESPONDENCE

CORRect your CORResponDENce in the DEN.

DEFINITELY

Find the word FINITE within.

DELIBERATE

It was a deLIBERATE plan
to LIBERATE the hostages.

DESPERATE

Imagine Desperate DESPERADOS!

DESERT (as in Sahara)
or DESSERT (as in crème brûlée)

Remember that the sweet one has two SugarS
or that the double 's' in 'dessert' stands for 'Sweet Stuff'.

DIARRHOEA

If you need to know how to spell this – here goes!

Dash **I**n **A R**eal **R**ush, **H**urry **O**r **E**lse **A**ccident!

DOUBT

Sometimes it's only natural to **B**e in doubt.

DRAUGHT

Think of **A**n **U**npleasant **G**ale **H**owling
Through the draughty corridors.

ECCENTRIC

The word literally means 'off centre',
so imagine an eccentric **C**razy **C**at
running round in circles.

ECZEMA

It's pronounced with an X,
but there's no X factor with this problem:
Even **C**lean **ZE**alots **MA**y get eczema.

EMBARRASS

Do you go **R**eally **R**ed **A**nd **S**mile **S**hyly
when embarrassed?

EXAGGERATE

If he's br**AGG**ing then he's surely exaggerating.

FASCINATE

Are you faSCInated by SCIence?

FORTY

Life begins when you can't spell your age.
FORget the 'u' in four when you spell FORty.

FRIEND

FRIEs are for sharing with your friend.

FULFIL

It's 'full' and 'fill', but with one L in each, not two.

GEOGRAPHY

General Eisenhower's Oldest Girl
Rode A Pony Home Yesterday.

GRAMMAR

There's no 'e' in grammar,
so think of GrandMA, who writes and speaks
with perfect grammar.

HANDKERCHIEF

It's shortened to 'hanky', but the long form has a D.
Think of holding a handkerchief in your HAND.

HAEMORRHAGE

Help! **A**ccident, **EM**ergency – **O**ften **R**uins **R**outine
Hospital **A**ppointment.

HEARD OR HERD

If you heard something you used your EAR.
There are lots of animals in a herd, so there can't
be A single one on its own in this word.

HUMOROUS

The root is humour,
but think of the humorous way
Americans spell HUMOR.

INDISPENSABLE

They say that no one is indispensable,
but only the most ABLE are indispensABLE.

INTERRUPT

It's a fact that it's **R**eally **R**ude to interrupt.

JEWELLERY

It's easy to forget the third E, but always remember
a JewELLER makes JewELLERy.

Just to confuse, Americans use jewelry and jeweler,
which are spelt as they sound, but break the above rule.

JODHPURS

These are tight-fitting trousers worn when
horse-riding, named after the city in India.
The silent H between the D and the P stands for Horse.

LIAISON

Dangerous – and misspelt
– if you don't use your two eyes = 2 Is.

MANOEUVRE

Sounds like hard work – it is MAN, short for manual,
and *OEUVRE*, a French word often meaning a work by
a composer, particularly opera.

MEMENTO

Commonly misspelt as 'momento'.
A souvenir from your holiday is a memento
and it represents happy MEMories.

MILLENNIUM

A thousand years – MILLE –
that's more than Ninety-Nine years.

MINIATURE

It means tiny and there are tiny words
in the middle – I and A.

MISSISSIPPI

The great river – a momentous word.

Mrs M, Mrs I, Mrs S S I, Mrs S S I,
Mrs P P I – Mississippi.

MISSPELL

The subject of this section of the book.
Don't miSS that extra 's' in miSSpell.

NECESSARY

Not Every Cat Eats Sardines –
Some Are Really Yummy.

Never Eat Crisps; Eat Salad Sandwiches
And Remain Young.

Or think of a shirt – it is necessary
for a shirt to have one Collar and two Sleeves.

Or think of a coffee – one Cream and two Sugars.

OCCASION

If it's a special one, you'd travel over two seas (Cs).

OCEAN

Only Cats' Eyes Are Narrow.

PARALLEL

There are three Ls in parallel, but think of the middle ones acting as parallel lines next to each other.

PARLIAMENT

Think I AM parliament.

PEOPLE

People Eat Other People's Leftovers Eagerly.

PNEUMONIA

People Never Expect Us to go down with PNEUmonia.

POSSESSION

Very sweet – four Sugars.

POTASSIUM

One Tea and two Sugars

PRINCIPAL or PRINCIPLE

A princiPAL can be your PAL,
and a principLE you believe is a ruLE.

Adjective or noun?
If it's an adjective it's princiPAL.

RHYTHM

Rhythm **H**elps **Y**ou **T**o **H**ear **M**usic.

Rhythm **H**elps **Y**our **T**wo **H**ips **M**ove.

RECOMMEND

No need for confusion with this word.
It's simply 'commend' with RE at the beginning.

RIDICULOUS

This word is derived from RIDICULE.
Remember this and you'll never put an E in it.

SEPARATE

It's so common to see this word spelt 'seperate' instead of
'separate'. Just think of your old Father or PA in his den,
as a sePArate kind of person.

STATIONERY or STATIONARY

A or E? Every office junior gets the spelling of this word
wrong at least once in their life. You only have to
remember one, and by process of elimination the other
must be right! Think of the initial 'e' in 'envelope' for
'stationery', or keep in mind the following sentences:

PEns are items of stationEry

CArs when parked are stationAry

SUBTLE

To Be subtle – Be silent.

SUCCEED

Succeed, Proceed, Exceed
are the only three English words that end in CEED.
Take the initial letters of these words
and think SPEED.

———

SUPERSEDE

There is no 'c' in supersede, but there is a second 's'.
It's the only word in the dictionary that ends SEDE.
All the others containing CEDE end like this,
e.g. precede, recede.

———

THERE *or* THEIR

Think directions for THERE:
it's either HERE or THERE.
HERE is over THERE,
and can be found in THERE.

Think of ownership for THEIR:
someone is an HEIR before they inherit
THEIR fortune.

———

TOGETHER

Split it up into three separate words:
think TO GET HER.

WEATHER or WHETHER

WE look AT HER (the TV weather girl)
to check the forecast and discover whether
it will be sunny or rainy.

WEDNESDAY

WE Do Not Eat Soup DAY.

WOOLLY

W, Double-O, Double-L, Y

This works for 'coolly' as well.
Resist the temptation to spell with one L.

YOU'RE or YOUR

YOU'RE never going to get it right
if you don't use YOUR head.

If something belongs to us, it is OURs,
just as something that belongs to you is YOURs.

3
Think of a Number

First Steps: Counting Rhymes

Learning to count is the first step to understanding arithmetic. Most of us do it with nursery rhymes, which contain the essential ingredients of mnemonics: imagery, rhyme and fun. Nursery rhymes are one of the first mnemonic devices we encounter as children. 'One, Two, Buckle My Shoe' was devised many years ago as a fun way to teach children how to count to twenty using rhyme and imagery. Here are two slightly different versions of the famous verse:

> One, Two, buckle my shoe,
> Three, Four, knock at the door,
> Five, Six, pick up sticks,
> Seven, Eight, lay them straight,
> Nine, Ten, a big fat hen,
> Eleven, Twelve, dig and delve,
> Thirteen, Fourteen, maids a-courting,
> Fifteen, Sixteen, maids in the kitchen,
> Seventeen, Eighteen, maids in waiting,
> Nineteen, Twenty, my plate's empty.

> One, Two, buckle my shoe,
> Three, Four, knock at the door,
> Five, Six, pick up sticks,
> Seven, Eight, don't be late,
> Nine, Ten, a good fat hen,
> Eleven, Twelve, dig and delve
> Thirteen, Fourteen, maids a-courting,
> Fifteen, Sixteen, maids a-kissing,
> Seventeen, Eighteen, maids a-waiting,
> Nineteen, Twenty, I've had plenty.

'One, Two, Three, Four, Five', which is also known as 'Once I Caught a Fish Alive', is another famous counting rhyme. Though its origins are unknown, its earliest date of publication has been traced back to 1888:

> One, two, three, four, five.
> Once I caught a fish alive.
> Six, seven, eight, nine, ten.
> Then I let it go again.
> Why did you let it go?
> Because it bit my finger so.
> Which finger did it bite?
> This little finger on my right.

This shorter counting rhyme was also popular with children:

> One, Two, Three, Four,
> Mary's at the cottage door.
> Five, Six, Seven, Eight,
> Eating cherries off a plate.

Writing Numbers

Mastering the numbers out loud is one thing, but writing them down is something else entirely. However, this number-writing poem doubtless helped countless youngsters:

Around to the left to find my hero,
Back to the top, I've made a zero.

Downward stroke, my that's fun,
Now I've made the number 1.

Half a heart says, 'I love you.'
A line – now I made the number 2.

Around the tree, around the tree,
Now I've made the number 3.

Down and across and down once more
Now I've made the number 4.

The hat, the back, the belly – a 5.
Watch out! It might come alive.

Bend down low to pick up sticks,
Now I've made the number 6.

Across the sky, and down from heaven,
Now I've made the number 7.

Make an 'S' and close the gate,
Now I've made the number 8.

An oval and a line,
Now I've made the number 9.

One (1) egg (0) laid my hen.
Now I've made the number 10.

Roman Numerals

Imagine doing sums using Roman numerals. They are still used today for indicating successive same-name kings, queens, sons and daughters, movie sequels and dates, and also for successive Olympic Games and the Super Bowl, but their usage is quite rare. I, V and X are more commonly used, particularly on clock faces, so we are generally more familiar with these numerals and the fact that they represent 1, 5 and 10 respectively. It's a good idea to remember that C stands for 'century', i.e. 100 years:

I	V	X	L	C	D	M
1	5	10	50	100	500	1,000

The Romans did not have a notation for zero, which meant that early in the second millennium the system was gradually replaced by the Arabic numerals that we use today. As Roman numerals are considerably under-used in modern society, there's a danger that we might start to forget them, so here's a simple mnemonic to help keep the system in mind:

I Value **X**ylophones **L**ike **C**ows **D**ig **M**ilk

If you can only remember the first three letters IVX, you could recite the following to recall LCD and M:

Lucy **C**an't **D**rink **M**ilk

This poem is useful for learning Roman numerals:

X shall stand for playmates Ten,
V for Five stout stalwart men,
I for One as I'm alive,
C for Hundred and D for Five,
M for a Thousand soldiers true,
And L for Fifty, I'll tell you.

As is this pithy verse:

M's mille – or 1,000 said,
D's half – 500 quickly read.
C's just a 100 – century
And L is half again – 50.
So all that's left is X and V
Or 10 and 5 and I is easy.

The Metric System

Metrication, or the decimal system, began in France in the 1790s, and even today the rest of the world is still catching up. In Britain and the USA, we still measure our journeys in miles, but in the fields of building, science and engineering we've been fully metricated.

Kilometre	1,000 metres
Hectometre	100 metres
Decametre	10 metres
Metre (base)	1 metre

Deci**metre**	¹⁄₁₀ of a metre
Centi**metre**	¹⁄₁₀₀ of a metre
Milli**metre**	¹⁄₁₀₀₀ of a metre

The first letters stand for the metric prefixes and base unit: Kilo, Hecto, Deca, Metre (base), Deci, Centi, Milli. The following phrases help to remember the correct order:

King Henry Died Mightily Drinking Chocolate Milk

Kippers Hardly Dare Move During Cold Months

King Henry Died – Mother Didn't Care Much

King Hector Died Miserable Death – Caught Measles

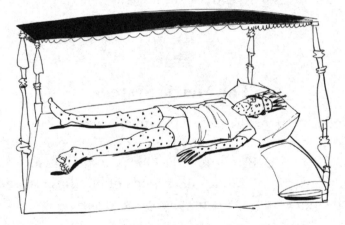

If the base unit is a gram rather than a metre we would have:

King Henry Died – Granny Didn't Care Much

Times-Table Tricks

Ten-Times Table

We all know that to multiply a number by ten we simply add a zero to it. This is a mnemonic device. 3 x 10 = 30 just as 26,350 x 10 = 263,500. As the numbers get larger, it is just a simple task of adding a zero and moving the comma along to the right by one place.

Nine-Times Table

There are an infinite number of patterns to be found in arithmetic, particularly in the nine-times table.

$9 \times 1 = 9$	$9 \times 6 = 54$
$9 \times 2 = 18$	$9 \times 7 = 63$
$9 \times 3 = 27$	$9 \times 8 = 72$
$9 \times 4 = 36$	$9 \times 9 = 81$
$9 \times 5 = 45$	$9 \times 10 = 90$

Halfway through the nine-times table at 5, see how the numbers invert, i.e.:

$$9 \times 5 = 45; 9 \times 6 = 54$$

Up to 9 × 10, notice how the digits in the products of numbers multiplied by 9 always add up to 9, i.e.:

$$9 \times 2 = 18 \, (1 + 8 = 9), 9 \times 3 = 27 \, (2 + 7 = 9).$$

Nine-Times Table: By Hand

How many of us learned this cunning way to remember our nine-times table, using only our hands?

Firstly, hold your two hands up with the palms facing you, and number each digit from 1 to 10, starting with the thumb on your left hand (1) through to the thumb on your right hand (10).

For 9 × 2, you need to bend digit number 2 (your left index finger) to signify 'times 2'. This leaves your thumb (1) outstretched to the left of your bent index finger, and 8 digits outstretched to the right of it. Put 1 and 8 together to make the sum of 9 × 2.

For 9 × 6, you need to bend digit number 6 (your right pinky) to represent 'times 6'. This leaves all the digits on your left hand outstretched (5) and the remaining digits on your right hand outstretched (4). Put 5 and 4 together to make the sum of 9 × 6.

You look at the number of fingers to the left side of the folded-down finger to find out what number is in the tens column of the answer, and you look to the right of the folded-down finger to find the number in the ones column. It couldn't be simpler!

Long Division

When it comes to the technique for remembering which steps to follow when doing long division – **D**ivide, **M**ultiply, **S**ubtract, **B**ring down – use one of these memorable phrases:

Dad, **M**um, **S**ister, **B**rother

Dead **M**onkeys **S**mell **B**ad

The Order of Calculation

The order we must use to work out a sum is: **M**ultiply and **D**ivide before you **A**dd and **S**ubtract. Any mathematical statement with an 'equals' sign is an equation, i.e. one side of the equation equals the other side. For example, $1 + 1 = 2$ is an equation, just as $2 \times 10 = 4 \times 5$ is an equation.

Some people find that the following phrase helps them remember the MDAS correct order:

My **D**ear **A**unt **S**ally

When things get a bit more complicated, and there are several functions to work out in a sum, the PEMDAS way is the order in which to tackle the problem:

Parentheses **E**xponents **M**ultiplication
Division **A**ddition **S**ubtraction

Certain phrases are useful for keeping the correct order in mind:

Please **E**xcuse **M**y **D**ear **A**unt **S**ally

Please **E**xecute **M**y **D**og **A**nd **S**oon

Put **E**very **M**an **D**own **A**nd **S**hout

Others will have been taught the **BIDMAS** alternative, which works in exactly the same way.

Brackets **I**ndices **D**ivision **M**ultiplication
Addition **S**ubtraction

BIDMAS allows you to calculate the sum written as:

$$(8 - 3) \times 4 + \frac{15}{5} - 3 = 20$$

The B for Brackets in BIDMAS means the same as the P for Parentheses in PEMDAS, as does the I for Indices and the E for Exponents. The order of Division and Multiplication is flexible, so the order can either be DM or MD.

Finding Averages

Here is an excellent way to remember the names of the four methods of finding averages, using the '**Medi**um-**Range Mean Model**' method:

Median – the number exactly in the middle when a set of numbers is listed in order.

Range – the difference between the highest and lowest numbers in a set.

Mean – the sum of a set of numbers, divided by the number of numbers in the set.

Mode – the number (or numbers) that appears most frequently in a set.

Isosceles Triangles

To help distinguish between an isosceles triangle and all other types of triangle, this song sung to the tune of 'Oh, Christmas Tree' has proved a valuable aid:

> Oh, isosceles, oh, isosceles,
> Two angles have
> Equal degrees.
> Oh, isosceles, oh, isosceles,
> You look just like
> A Christmas tree.

Dividing by Fractions

A fraction is a numerical quantity that is not a whole number, for example ½ or ¹⁹⁄₂₀, which are quantities that form part of a whole.

The definition of a fraction is a numerator divided by a denominator, but which is which?

Think of 'Notre Dame':

NUmerator **U**p, **D**enominator **D**own.

Therefore, in ½, 1 is the numerator, 2 is the denominator. In ¹⁹⁄₂₀, 19 is the numerator, 20 is the denominator.

This rhyme will help every student who gets into a muddle when dividing by fractions:

> The number you're dividing by,
> Turn upside down and multiply.

> e.g. 10 divided by ½ = 10 × ²⁄₁ = 20
> or 15 divided by ⅕ = 15 × ⁵⁄₁ = 75

The Value of Pi

Pi is the Greek letter π. It is a mathematical constant and calculated as the ratio of the circumference of a circle to its diameter. Pi is the number 3.14159, although in reality it has an infinite number of decimal places.

The traditional way to remind yourself of the decimals is to use phrases containing word-length mnemonics, where the number of letters in each word corresponds to a digit.

Pi to six decimal places is:

How I wish I could calculate pi = 3.141592

And to fourteen places:

How I like a drink,
alcoholic of course,
after the heavy lectures involving
quantum mechanics = 3.14159265358979

And here's a rhyme to twenty decimal places of pi:

Now, I wish I could recollect pi.
'Eureka,' cried the great inventor.
Christmas Pudding, Christmas Pie,
Is the problem's very centre.
= 3.14159265358979323846

And to thirty-one decimal places:

Sir, I bear a rhyme excelling
In mystic force, and magic spelling
Celestial sprites elucidate
All my own striving can't relate
Or locate they who can cogitate
And so finally terminate. Finis.
= 3.1415926535897932384626433832795

This useful method of remembering pi only works up to thirty-one decimal places, unfortunately, because the thirty-second number after the decimal point is 0.

From *Omni,* the celebrated science magazine of the late 1970s and early 1980s, this is a fun verse devised to help students to calculate the circumference of a circle using pi:

> If you cross a circle with a line,
> Which hits the centre and runs from spine to spine,
> And the line's length is d
> The circumference will be d times 3.14159.

The area of a circle is calculated as π × r-squared (where r is the radius) = πr².

To help remember the formula, think:

> Apple Pie Are Square.

The circumference of a circle is calculated as π × d (where d is the diameter) = πd.

One memorable way to recall the formula is to think:

> Cherry Pie Delicious.

The following rhyme can help us to learn the difference between circumference and area:

> Fiddlededum, fiddlededee,
> A ring round the moon is π times d,
> If a hole in your sock you want repaired,
> You use the formula πr-squared.

Square Roots

Just as subtraction is the opposite of addition and division is the opposite of multiplication, so square roots are the opposite of squaring, i.e. multiplying a number by itself, so the square root of 4 is 2, i.e. $2 \times 2 = 4$.

This is a perfect square root and is therefore quite simple. Things get more interesting when maths explores more complicated concepts such as the square root of 2. Which number multiplied by itself makes 2? It's not a round number and so, as with pi, the length of each word in the following rhymes represents each digit:

> For the square root of 2,
> I wish I knew
> 1.414 – the root of two.

> For the square root of 3,
> O, charmed was he
> 1.732 – to know the root of three.

> For the square root of 5,
> So we now strive
> 2.236 – to know the root of five.

> For the square root of 6
> We need more logistics
> 2.449 – to know the root of six.

Pythagoras' Theorem

Pythagoras (*c.*580–500 BC) was a Greek mathematician and philosopher from Samos, sometimes known as 'The Father of Numbers'. His famous theorem is a maths standard that reveals how to calculate the lengths of the three sides of a right-angled triangle.

In essence, Pythagoras' theorem states that the square of the hypotenuse is equal to the sum of the squares of the other two sides, or HYPOTENUSE squared = BASE squared + HEIGHT squared.

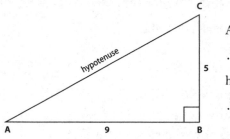

$AB = 9$ cm $BC = 5$ cm

$\therefore 9^2 + 5^2 = 106$

$hyp = \sqrt{106} = 10.3$ cm

$\therefore 10.3$ cm$^2 = 9$ cm$^2 + 5$ cm^2

To help maths students remember the formula, a visual aid in the form of the 'teepee story' was devised, which featured a memorable mnemonic punchline:

A Red Indian chief had three squaws in three teepees. When he came home late from hunting, he never knew which squaw was in which teepee because it was always dark. One day he killed a hippopotamus, a bear and a buffalo. He put one hide from each animal into each teepee, so that when he came home late he could feel inside the teepee and he would know which squaw was which. After a year, all three squaws had had children. The squaw on the bear hide had a baby boy, the squaw on the buffalo hide had a baby girl. But the squaw on the hippopotamus hide had a girl and a boy. And the moral of the story?

The squaw on the hippopotamus is equal to the sum of the squaws on the other two hides.

Trigonometry: Sine Cosine Tangent

By definition, triangles are all about threes – sides and angles. If you know two elements of a right-angled triangle, whether it be sides, angles or one of each, you can then work out the third.

In a right-angled triangle, if the value of a second angle is given:

the **S**ine of the angle = the ratio of the **O**pposite side to the **H**ypotenuse

the **C**osine of the angle = the ratio of the **A**djacent side to the **H**ypotenuse

the **T**angent of the angle = the ratio of the **O**pposite and the **A**djacent sides

For example, in this diagram,

$$\sin (A) = \frac{a}{c}$$

$$\cos (A) = \frac{b}{c}$$

$$\tan (A) = \frac{a}{b}$$

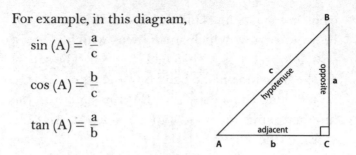

The initials spell **SOH–CAH–TOA**, which is easy to recall because it rhymes with Krakatoa, the volcanic island in Indonesia. If, however, the volcano comparison is less than effective, one of the examples below might prove more memorable:

Smiles **O**f **H**appiness **C**ome
After **H**aving **T**ankards **O**f **A**le

Some **O**ld **H**ag **C**aught
A **H**ippy **T**ripping **O**n **A**cid

Some **O**ld **H**orse **C**aught **A**nother **H**orse
Taking **O**ats **A**way

Graph Co-ordinates

From simple bar charts showing hours of sunshine against months of the year to advanced calculus graphs indicating rates of change, this is the rule for all graphs:

X along the corridor,
Y up and down the stairs.

The convention for labelling a pair of coordinates (x and y) is that x is the horizontal shift and y the vertical shift.

Converting Miles to Kilometres

Fibonacci numbers are named after the thirteenth-century mathematician Leonardo of Pisa, who was also called Leonardo Fibonacci. They are whole numbers in sequence: 0, 1, 1, 2, 3, 5, 8, 13, 21, 34, 55, 89 . . . and so on to infinity. Each number in the series is the sum of the previous two numbers.

There are approximately 8 (8.05 km) kilometres in 5 miles, and since both 8 and 5 are Fibonacci numbers, you can convert kilometres to miles and miles to kilometres by looking at the consecutive numbers. Just remember there will always be more kilometres (longer word) than miles (shorter word).

$$8 \text{ km} = 5 \text{ miles}$$
$$13 \text{ km} = 8 \text{ miles}$$
$$21 \text{ km} = 13 \text{ miles}$$
$$34 \text{ km} = 21 \text{ miles}$$
$$55 \text{ km} = 34 \text{ miles}$$
$$89 \text{ km} = 55 \text{ miles}$$

4
Geographically Speaking

━━━━━

Learning Directions

When we first learn about geography and the places around us, we're taught the four main compass directions: North, South, East and West. Remembering exactly where these points are on a compass should be quite straightforward, but to avoid memory loss, a number of useful phrases have been devised.

Firstly, you can use the acronym NEWS:

North at the top
East on the right
West on the left
South at the bottom

Alternatively, the first letters of each word in these sentences indicate the points of the compass in clockwise order:

Never **E**at **S**hredded **W**heat

Never **E**at **S**limy **W**orms
Never **E**nter **S**anta's **W**orkshop
Never **E**at **S**oggy **W**affles
Naughty **E**lephants **S**quirt **W**ater

Latitude and Longitude

If you've ever had problems remembering which direction latitude and longitude lines go, here are a few mnemonic pointers to ensure you'll never be bamboozled again.

The Latin word *latus* means 'side', hence latitude lines go from side to side.

The phrase 'Lat is fat' should help remind us that the central lines of latitude go around the 'belt' of the equator.

Longitude lines seem *long*er, going from top to bottom or North to South.

The Tropics of Cancer and Capricorn

These are two imaginary lines running parallel to the equator (the longest line of latitude that spans the centre of the globe), which are based on the sun's position in relation to the earth at two points of the year. The sun is directly overhead at noon on the Tropic of Cancer on 21 June (the beginning of summer in the Northern Hemisphere and of winter in the Southern Hemisphere) and is again overhead at midday on the Tropic of Capricorn on 21 December (the beginning of winter in the Northern Hemisphere and of summer in the Southern Hemisphere).

The Tropic of Cancer lies 23.5° north of the equator and the Tropic of Capricorn lies at 23.5° south, and the following verse has helped many to remember this fact.

CaNcer lies North of the equator
CapricOrn lies on the Other side of the equator

Map Reading

Imagine you're a Girl Guide or Boy Scout on an expedition carrying no more than a bit of Kendal Mint Cake and an Ordnance Survey map, or a soldier in the field armed with just a map and a compass. Your map grid reference is 123456. To find your position on the map just think: 'Onwards and Upwards'.

Split your map reference into two sets of three figures: 123 and 456.

1 is the number of the grid line on the map going across – ONWARD – from west to east. 2 and 3 give more precise coordinates within that grid.

The 4 is the grid line going up – UPWARDS – from south to north. And 5 and 6 give a more precise location.

The Seven Continents of the World

A continent is defined as a large continuous land mass, and geographers state that the world has seven of them:

Europe   Asia   Africa   Australia
Antarctica   North America   South America

Although Europe is joined to Asia, the two areas are recognized as separate continents, with the Ural Mountains in Russia dividing the areas that we regard as East and West. Australia is the smallest continent, and also known as Oceania. Australia itself is an island of just under 3 million square miles. Asia is the largest continent at approximately 17 million square miles.

The following phrases are the most popular to remember the continents:

Eat An Aspirin After A Nasty Sandwich
Eat An Apple As A Nice Snack

The Great Lakes of North America

The five Great Lakes are, from west to east, Superior, Michigan, Huron, Erie and Ontario. As SMHEO is a less than memorable acronym, these short pithy sentences are far more effective:

Sally Made Henry Eat Onions
Sergeant-Major Hates Eating Oranges
Super Mario Heaved Earth Out

From east to west, try:

Old Elephants Have Much Skin

An easier and more commonly used mnemonic acronym is HOMES, but this jumbles up the correct geographical order.

Niagara Falls

Lenor is a fabric softener, but the letters in the word can also be used to remind us of which two great lakes surround Niagara Falls. Picture the scene as if looking at a map where north is at the top of the page.

Left – Erie – Niagara – Ontario – Right

The Countries of Central America

There are seven Central American countries, namely: **G**uatemala, **B**elize, **H**onduras, **E**l Salvador, **N**icaragua, **C**osta Rica and **P**anama. If these names or the letters GBHENCP don't roll easily off the tongue, try using this mnemonic phrase to jog your memory:

Great **B**ig **H**ungry **E**lephants
Nearly **C**onsumed **P**anama

The World's Longest Rivers

An unusual acronym used to remember the names of the world's longest rivers is NAYY CLAIM. The exact length of the two greatest rivers on earth, the Nile and the Amazon, varies over time and geographers disagree on their actual length. Therefore, this acronym is more of an aid to remembering the names of the rivers, rather than their exact pecking order, about which no one seems able to agree.

RIVER	CONTINENT	LENGTH
Nile	Africa	6,695 km (4,160 miles)
Amazon	South America	6,683 km (4,153 miles)
Yangtze (Chang Jiang)	Asia	6,380 km (3,964 miles)
Yellow (Huang Ho)	Asia	4,830 km (3,001 miles)
Congo (Zaire)	Africa	4,630 km (2,877 miles)
Lena	Asia	4,400 km (2,734 miles)
Amur (Heilong Jiang)	Asia	4,350 km (2,703 miles)
Irtysh	Asia	4,248 km (2,640 miles)
Mekong	Asia	4,180 km (2,597 miles)

The three longest rivers in Europe can be recalled using the acronym VDU (think Visual Display Unit):

RIVER	COUNTRY OF ORIGIN	LENGTH
Volga	Russia	3,688 km (2,292 miles)
Danube	Germany	2,850 km (1,771 miles)
Ural	Russia	2,428 km (1,509 miles)

The Counties of Northern Ireland

On a far smaller scale than the countries of Central America, the six counties of Northern Ireland are:

Armagh, **D**own, **A**ntrim, **L**ondonderry,
Tyrone and **F**ermanagh.

If you look at a diagram of the counties, beginning with Armagh going anticlockwise round to Fermanagh, you could remember this nonsense phrase:

Ants **D**rift **A**nticlockwise **L**onger **T**han **F**leas

It might even be easier to remember an anagram of the initial letters in no particular order, such as DAFT LA or FLAT DA.

The Rivers of the Pennines

During one hot summer, while studying geographical facts for school, I made up my own mnemonic nonsense word, SUNWACD, which comprised the initials of the rivers of the Pennines that all flow east into the River Ouse in Yorkshire:

Swale, **U**re, **N**idd, **W**harfe, **A**ire, **C**alder, **D**on.

The Seven Hills of Rome

Rome was built on the seven hills east of the River Tiber. Clockwise from the westernmost hill, they are **C**apitoline, **Q**uirinal, **V**iminal, **E**squiline, **C**aelian, **A**ventine and **P**alatine, and can be easily remembered with the following phrase:

Can **Q**ueen **V**ictoria **E**at **C**old **A**pple **P**ie?

Alternatively, if you start with the Quirinal, going in a clockwise direction, you could try remembering a slightly more amusing alternative:

Queen **V**ictoria **E**yes **C**aesar's **A**wfully **P**ainful **C**orns.

An even more memorable acronym is **PACE QVC**. *Pace* is the Italian word for 'peace' paired with QVC, the shopping channel.

Italian Geography

If you ever needed a reminder of the location of Sicily, here's a verse guaranteed to help:

Long-legged Italy kicked little Sicily
Right into the middle of the Mediterranean Sea.

5
Animal, Vegetable, Mineral

═══

Geological Periods

The list below details the geological classification of rock deposits, starting with the Cambrian, the first period in the Palaeozoic era.

	Approximate number of years ago
Cambrian	570–510 million
Ordovician	510–439 million
Silurian	439–409 million
Devonian	409–363 million
Carboniferous	363–290 million
Permian	290–245 million
Triassic	245–208 million
Jurassic	208–146 million
Cretaceous	146–65 million
Palaeocene	65–56.5 million
Eocene	56.5–35.4 million
Oligocene	35.4–23.3 million
Miocene	23.3–5.2 million
Pliocene	5.2–1.64 million

| Pleistocene | 1,640,000–10,000 |
| Recent (Holocene) | 10,000–present day |

Large mammals flourished and became extinct as recently as the Pleistocene period, during which time anatomically modern humans began to evolve. The Recent period marked the end of the last Ice Age and the start of the development of modern civilization.

Here's a memorable phrase to help you tell your Eocene from your Pliocene geological period, starting with the Cambrian era from over 500 million years ago:

Camels Often Sit Down Carefully.
Perhaps Their Joints Creak? Possibly Early Oiling
Might Prevent Permanent Rheumatism.

Components of Soil

When testing the soil for its age, geologists also need to know the main constituents of soil, namely **A**ir, **H**umus, **M**ineral salts, **W**ater, **B**acteria and **R**ock particles, which can be remembered with this jaunty saying:

All **H**airy **M**en **W**ill **B**uy **R**azors

The Hardness of Minerals

The Mohs Scale was devised in 1822 by German mineralogist Friedrich Mohs (1773–1839). He chose ten familiar, easily available minerals, and arranged them in order of their 'scratch hardness'.

Minerals in order from softest to hardest are:

1. **T**alc
2. **G**ypsum
3. **C**alcite
4. **F**luorite (fluorspar)
5. **A**patite
6. **O**rthoclase (feldspar)
7. **Q**uartz
8. **T**opaz
9. **C**orundum
10. **D**iamond

Groups 1–2 can be scratched by a fingernail.
Groups 3–6 can be scratched with a blade.
Groups 7–10 are hard enough to scratch glass.

A couple of mnemonics that some might find useful to memorize the Mohs Scale are:

Tall **G**irls **C**an **F**lirt **A**nd **O**ther **Q**ueer **T**hings
Can **D**evelop

TAll **GY**roscopes **CA**n **FL**y **AP**art **OR**biting
QUickly **TO** **CO**mplete **DI**sintegration

Types of Fossils

One way of learning the different types of fossils is to remember the acronym IMAP, which stands for:

Imprint
Moulds (or casts)
Actual remains
Petrified

Or keep in mind the following apt phrase:

I Marvel **At P**etrification

Stalactites and Stalagmites

Stalactites are formed when water containing calcium carbonate dissolves after seeping down through limestone or chalk, and evaporates leaving deposits of carbonates of lime to build up over time to form mineral columns in caves. Stalagmites develop in the same way when rain falls onto the floor of caves and minerals build up to form pillars.

The similarity between the spelling and pronunciation of the two words has confused many over the years, and so several memory aids have been developed to help simplify matters.

This example relies on the difference in spelling, using the C and the G to relate to the origin of the formation:

StalaCtites are formed on the Ceiling

StalaGmites are formed on the Ground

A slightly cheekier way is to think of the reaction to having ants (mites) in your pants:

The 'mites go up and the 'tites come down!

A couple of other suggestions have been:

Stalactites hang *tight* from the roof;
Stalagmites *might* reach the roof.

Stalactites hang down like *tight*s on a washing line;
Stalagmites *might* bite if you sit on them.

Camels: One Lump or Two

There are two main types of camel – one has one hump and the other has two. But what's the best way of remembering which is which?

A **B**actrian camel's back is shaped like the letter B
– it has two humps.

A **D**romedary's back is shaped like the letter D
– it only has one hump.

Both species of camel are natives of the dry deserts of Asia and North Africa. The Bactrian or two-humped camel inhabits central Asia. The Dromedary or one-humped camel is a light and fast breed, otherwise known as the Arabian Camel. The name derives from the Greek word *dromas* – to run. The Dromedary is domesticated and no longer lives in the wild.

Elephants Never Forget

How do you tell the difference between an Indian elephant and an African elephant? It's all in the size, as this rhyme proves:

India's big, and its elephant there features,
But Africa's bigger with much bigger creatures.

Generally the ears of an African elephant are bigger than those of its Indian counterpart. Imagine that they resemble the shape of the larger African continent, while those of the Indian elephant are the shape of India.

Insect Stings

From one of the world's largest creatures to two of the smallest. What home remedies are there if you are stung by a bee or a wasp?

> Use **A**mmonia for a **B**ee sting,
>
> And **V**inegar for a **W**asp sting
>
> **B** follows **A** and **W** follows **V**.
> (Think of the VW car as well.)

This is also a useful mnemonic with which to remember the Latin family classification of bees and wasps.

> **A**poidia are **B**ees
>
> **V**espidae are **W**asps

More correctly, the *apoidia* classification refers to the 'superfamily' of bees, while *vespidae* is the 'family' classification for wasps.

Taxonomic Classifications

Not to be confused with taxidermy, which is the art of preparing, stuffing and mounting animal skins, alpha taxonomy is the principle of arranging groups of living organisms, i.e. plants and animals, into groups based on similarities of structure and origin. To give an example of the classifications, here are the definitions of man or *homo sapiens*:

Kingdom	*Animalia*
Phylum	*Vertibrata*
Class	*Mammalia*
Order	*Primate*
Family	*Hominidae*
Genus	*Homo*
Species	*Sapiens*
Variety	—

To remember the different classifications including 'variety', these two phrases roll off the tongue nicely:

Krakatoa **P**ositively **C**asts **O**ff **F**umes **G**enerating **S**ulphurous **V**apours

Kindly **P**lace **C**over **O**n **F**resh **G**reen **S**pring **V**egetables

Versions excluding any reference to 'variety' can be remembered thus:

Kids **P**refer **C**heese **O**ver **F**ried **G**reen **S**pinach
King **P**hilip **C**ame **O**ver **F**or **G**ood **S**oup
King **P**hilip **C**ould **O**nly **F**ind **G**reen **S**ocks

Cedar Trees

Evergreen cedar trees in most British parks and gardens come in three types:

Atlas has Ascending branches

Lebanon has Level branches

Deodar has Drooping branches

The Mount Atlas cedar originates from the Atlas Mountains of Algeria and Morocco, and was introduced to Britain in 1841. The Lebanon cedar arrived in the UK in 1638 from the Middle East and was widely used by landscape designer Capability Brown in the eighteenth century. And the deodar (from the Sanskrit *deva dara* meaning 'divine tree') first came from the Himalayas.

Firewood

If you are laying a fire at home or making a campfire, bring this traditional poem to mind to avoid suffocating smoke and flying sparks:

Beech wood fires are bright and clear,
If the logs are kept a year.
Chestnut's only good, they say,
If for long it's laid away.
Birch and fir logs burn too fast,
Blaze up bright and do not last.

Elm wood burns like a churchyard mould,
Even the very flames are cold.
Poplar gives a bitter smoke,
Fills your eyes and makes you choke.
Apple wood will scent your room
With an incense like perfume.
Oak and maple, if dry and old,
Keep away the winter cold.
But ash wood wet and ash wood dry,
A king shall warm his slippers by.

6
Time and the Calendar

Spring Forward, Fall Back

The seasons change, the clocks go back and forth, time waits for no man, and woe betide if you forget to reset your clock at the beginning of autumn and spring. The end of summer time in Europe takes place at 1 a.m. on the fourth Sunday in October. Summer time begins again on the third Sunday in March. So in the **spring** we move our clocks **forward** one hour to herald summer and in autumn (or **fall**) we go **back** one hour to welcome winter.

A similar saying to 'Spring Forward, Fall Back' was created to remind people of the change in time: 'Forward April, back September. That is all you need to remember.'

'Thirty Days Hath September ...'

The words to this rhyme are possibly the most oft-repeated of all memory aids. How many of us, since learning the verse in childhood, still find ourselves muttering the lines to recall how many days there are in each month?

The origin of the 'Thirty Days Hath September' poem is obscure, but the use of 'olde' English in the verse suggests that it dates back to at least the sixteenth century. There are a couple of different endings to the last two lines of the verse that are both recorded below:

> Thirty days hath September,
> April, June and November;
> All the rest have thirty-one
> Excepting February alone,
> And that has twenty-eight days clear,
> With twenty-nine in each leap year.
>
> Which hath but twenty-eight, in fine,
> Till leap year gives it twenty-nine.

As the verse informs us that four particular months contain thirty days, and February has either twenty-eight or twenty-nine, by process of elimination we can work out that the remaining seven months all comprise thirty-one days. February was the last month in the Julian calendar year, which is why it is left to pick up the leftovers.

Days of the Months by Hand

A physical mnemonic trick that can help you work out the days of the months is right in front of you on the back of your hands. Place your clenched fists together, side by side, and begin with your left hand, naming the knuckle of your little finger as January. The valley or dip between the first two knuckles is February, the knuckle of the ring finger is March and the next valley is April. July marks the last knuckle on the left hand, and August marks the first knuckle on the right hand, as both months have thirty-one days. Carry on until you reach the penultimate knuckle on your right hand, representing December. The two thumb knuckles are both excluded from this technique.

All the knuckles represent months with thirty-one days and the valleys the shorter months. As in the rhyme above, we need to remember that February is the exception. So, if you can't remember the famous verse,

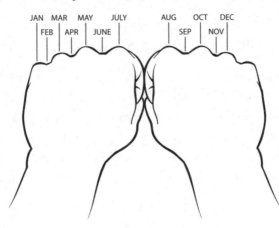

you can always rely on your own hands to jog your memory where the months of the year are concerned. If you're doing it in public, though, try not to make it obvious, otherwise you might attract some curious looks!

Quarter Days

By definition there are four quarter days in the year. Traditionally they were the four dates when rents and rates were due, particularly in rural districts, and also the days on which servants were hired. They coincided with four religious festivals and are about three months apart. Their importance is now limited, but in England the due dates for some leasehold payments and rents for businesses still fall on quarter days. They are:

25 March	5 letters in March – Lady Day (the feast of the Annunciation of Our Lady, the Virgin Mary) and New Year's Day in the Julian calendar
24 June	4 letters in June – Midsummer's Day
29 September	9 letters in September – Michaelmas Day
25 December	Christmas Day – everyone remembers that!

Bonfire Night

Being able to recall the date in 1605 when Guy Fawkes and his co-conspirators were caught trying to blow up the Houses of Parliament was made considerably easier with this snappy little rhyme:

> Remember, remember,
> The Fifth of November,
> Gunpowder, treason and plot.
> I know of no reason why the gunpowder treason
> Should ever be forgot.
> Guy Fawkes, Guy Fawkes, 'twas his intent
> To blow up the King and Parliament.
> Threescore barrels of powder below,
> Poor old England to overthrow;
> By God's providence he was catch'd
> With a dark lantern and burning match.

For plotting against the government, Guy Fawkes was subsequently tried as a traitor, and sentenced to death by being hanged, drawn and quartered. A year later it became an annual custom for the King and Parliament to deliver a sermon to commemorate the event, which also served as a warning to each new generation that treason was a heinous crime and one that incurred the most severe of punishments.

The British Gardening Calendar

Pruning encourages growth, so remember this rhyme for best results:

> Cut thistles in May,
> They'll grow in a day;
> Cut them in June,
> That's too soon;
> Cut them in July,
> Then they will die.

Time Travel

When travelling long distances throughout the world, it helps to remember EWG and WEL when calculating if you'll be losing or gaining time during a journey:

East to **W**est **G**ains and **W**est to **E**ast **L**oses.

The Caribbean Hurricane Season

The people of the Caribbean and the southern states of America are only too aware of the risks of hurricanes, as this mnemonic indicates:

June – Too Soon (first month)

July – Stand By (for any news of a storm)

August – You Must (prepare in case a storm comes)

September – Remember (to stand by)

October – It's All Over (last month)

The Signs of the Zodiac

Aries	The Ram	21 March – 20 April
Taurus	The Bull	21 April – 21 May
Gemini	The Twins	22 May – 22 June
Cancer	The Crab	23 June – 23 July
Leo	The Lion	21 July – 22 August
Virgo	The Virgin	24 August – 23 September
Libra	The Scales	24 September – 23 October
Scorpio	The Scorpion	24 October – 22 November
Sagittarius	The Archer	23 November – 21 December
Capricorn	The Goat	22 December – 20 January

| Aquarius | The Water Bearer | 21 January – 19 February |
| Pisces | The Fish | 20 February – 20 March |

The first letters of the words in this mnemonic sentence give us of the signs of the astrological zodiac in order, which can be remembered with these phrases:

All The Great Chancellors Live Very Long
Since Shops Can't Alter Politics

A Tense Grey Cat Lay Very Low
Sneaking Slowly, Contemplating A Pounce

Alternatively, if we start from January, we have Capricorn, Aquarius, Pisces, Aries, Taurus, Gemini, Cancer, Leo, Virgo, Libra, Scorpio, Sagittarius:

Can All People Always Take Good Care
Lighting Valuable Lamps Surrounding Salisbury?

If you are inclined to recall lists with a sense of rhythm instead, use the verse written by preacher, poet and hymn writer, Isaac Watts (1674–1748), which starts with Aries:

The *Ram*, the *Bull*, the heavenly *Twins*,
And next the *Crab*, the *Lion* shines,
The *Virgin* and the *Scales*;
The *Scorpion*, *Archer* and the *Goat*.
The *Man* who pours the water out
And *Fish* with glittering scales.

Or perhaps try this alternative from E. Cobham Brewer's
Dictionary of Phrase & Fable (1899):

> Our vernal signs the *Ram* begins
> Then comes the *Bull,* in May the *Twins;*
> The *Crab* in June, next *Leo* shines,
> And *Virgo* ends the northern signs.
> The *Balance* brings autumnal fruits,
> The *Scorpion* stings, the *Archer* shoots;
> December's *Goat* brings wintry blast,
> *Aquarius* rain, the *Fish* comes last.

7
The Sky at Night and by Day

The Order of the Planets

Before August 2006, the planets in our solar system were **M**ercury, **V**enus, **E**arth, **M**ars, **J**upiter, **S**aturn, **U**ranus, **N**eptune and **P**luto. Their initial letters lent themselves to all sorts of phrases:

My **V**ery **E**asy **M**ethod: **J**ust **S**et **U**p **N**ine **P**lanets

My **V**ery **E**ducated **M**other **J**ust **S**erved **U**s **N**ine **P**izzas

Mum's **V**ery **E**arly **M**orning **J**am **S**andwiches **U**sually **N**auseate **P**eople

In August 2006, the International Astronomical Union decided to downgrade the status of Pluto, and so some new mnemonic phrases that don't mention poor old Pluto have had to be devised for the new generation of stargazers:

My **V**ery **E**nergetic **M**other **J**ust **S**ent **U**s **N**owhere

My **V**ery **E**ducated **M**other **J**ust **S**ent **U**s **N**uts

My **V**ery **E**xotic **M**istress **J**ust **S**erved **U**s **N**oodles

The four planets closest to the sun are **M**ercury, **V**enus, **E**arth and **M**ars. These are called the 'rocky' or 'terrestrial' planets, and are small in relation to other planets while consisting of similar materials to earth:

My **V**isitor **E**ats **M**ice

My **V**irgin **E**ats **M**en

My **V**oice **E**xpects **M**ore

The 'gas' planets are **J**upiter, **S**aturn, **U**ranus and **N**eptune, which all have rings and moons, and consist mainly of hydrogen, helium, frozen water, ammonia, methane and carbon monoxide:

Jam **S**andwiches **U**sually **N**eeded

Jolly **S**usan's **U**nder-**N**ourished

John **S**mith **U**psets **N**eighbours

Saturn's Moons

Saturn has a number of moons (thirty-five have been named to date). To recall the nine principal moons of Saturn, think about how you MET DR THIP:

Mimas, **E**nceladus, **T**ethys, **D**ione, **R**hea, **T**itan, **H**yperion, **I**apetus, **P**hoebe

The Brightest Stars in the Sky

Positioned at the centre of the solar system, the closest star to earth is the sun. The brightest stars visible from earth are listed below, along with the constellation where each is located:

Sir Can Rig A VCR, PA

Sir	Sirius in Canis Major
Can	Canopus in Carina
Rig	Rigil Kent in Centaurus
A	Arcturus in Boötes
V	Vega in Lyra
C	Capella in Auriga
R	Rigel in Orion
P	Procyon in Canis Minor
A	Achernar in Eridanus

The Earth's Atmospheres

Troposphere: extends from the earth's surface to approximately 6–10 km.

Stratosphere: extends to approximately 10–50 km above earth.

Mesosphere: located 50–80 km above the earth's surface.

Thermosphere: located more than 80 km above earth.

Exosphere: the outermost layer of the atmosphere at 500–1,000 km above the earth.

To help recall the order of the earth's atmospheres, the following phrases may act as helpful reminders:

The **S**trong **M**an's **T**riceps **E**xplode

The **S**traight **M**an's **T**hrottle **E**xcites

Men on the Moon

Named after the Greek god of the sun, Project Apollo was a series of manned space flights that aimed to land a man on the moon by the end of the 1960s. This was eventually achieved by Neil Armstrong on 20 July 1969, when he became the first man to walk on the moon. Armstrong was a member of the crew of Apollo 11, which we can remember by the double 'll' in 'Apollo'. The names of Armstrong and his fellow astronauts can be recalled with a simple use of the ABC:

Neil **A**rmstrong

Buzz Aldrin

Michael **C**ollins

The Apollo programme lasted until only 1975 when it was cut short due to rising costs. Only twelve men have ever walked on the moon: Neil Armstrong, Buzz Aldrin, Pete Conrad, Alan Bean, Alan Shepard, Edgar Mitchell, David Scott, James Irwin, John W. Young, Charles Duke, Eugene Cernan and Harrison Schmitt.

Colours of the Rainbow

When a rainbow appears in the sky as a result of the refraction and dispersion of the sun's rays by light or other water droplets, the seven colours that are said to be visible are: **R**ed, **O**range, **Y**ellow, **G**reen, **B**lue, **I**ndigo and **V**iolet.

'**R**ichard **O**f **Y**ork **G**ave **B**attle **I**n **V**ain' is the popular mnemonic phrase with which most people are familiar. It refers to the Battle of Bosworth in 1485, when King Richard III was defeated by Henry Tudor, who became, as Henry VII, the first king of the Tudor dynasty. However, it can also be fun to make up other phrases such as:

Run **O**ff **Y**ou **G**irls, **B**oys **I**n **V**iew!

Roll **O**ut **Y**our **G**uinness, **B**oys **I**n **V**ats!

While some people prefer to recall the colours by making up a man's name: **ROY G BIV**.

Nowadays, however, it is widely believed that indigo does not strictly appear in the spectrum, but was merely included by Sir Isaac Newton, the seventeenth-century English physicist and mathematician, because seven colours was considered to be better than six.

Weather Forecasting

A red sky at night; shepherd's delight,
A red sky in the morning; shepherd's warning.

The origins of this rhyme can be traced back to St Matthew's Gospel in the Bible:

'When evening comes, you say, "It will be fair weather, for the sky is red", and in the morning, "Today it will be stormy, for the sky is red and overcast."'

In Britain the words refer to a shepherd who would say that a red sky in the morning would indicate inclement weather to follow, while in the USA the words relate to a sailor's predictions:

> Red sky at night, sailor's delight;
> Red sky at morning, sailor's warning.

Hundreds of years ago, before there were any accurate ways of weather forecasting, people had to rely on those with knowledge and experience, such as sailors and shepherds, whose lives were dependent on the weather and its changing moods.

Temperatures in Celsius

When Britain went metric in the 1970s and weather forecasters predicted the temperature in Celsius, it all got rather confusing. Here's a simple rhyme featuring different Celsius temperatures to help you decide whether to take a cardigan or an overcoat:

> 30°C is hot
>
> 20°C is nice
>
> 10°C is cold
>
> 0°C is ice

8

The World of Science

—————

During the course of their studies, chemistry students are expected to have a good knowledge of the names and properties of the 100+ chemical elements. It's crucial that they learn their unique properties and how they react with each other because getting it wrong can have disastrously flat, fizzy or fiery consequences.

The Periodic Table of Elements

The Periodic Table was devised in 1869 by Russian chemist Dmitri Mendeleyev. The elements are arranged in increasing order of atomic number from left to right across the table so that elements with a similar atomic structure and chemical properties appear in vertical columns. The horizontal rows are called periods and the vertical rows are known as groups.

Setting a long list of strange names to music is a tried and tested way to remember them. Music has a structure and flow, so if the words fit, they fly off the tongue with ease. Try replacing the lyrics of Gilbert and Sullivan's 'I Am the Very Model of a Modern Major-General' with the list of the chemical elements – as devised by Tom Lehrer – and you will never forget them:

There's antimony, arsenic, aluminium, selenium,
And hydrogen and oxygen and nitrogen and rhenium,
And nickel, neodymium, neptunium, germanium,
And iron, americium, ruthenium, uranium,
Europium, zirconium, lutetium, vanadium,
And lanthanum and osmium and astatine and radium,
And gold and protactinium and indium and gallium,

[Gasp.]

And iodine and thorium and thulium and thallium.
There's yttrium, ytterbium, actinium, rubidium,
And boron, gadolinium, niobium, iridium,
And strontium and silicon and silver and samarium,
And bismuth, bromine, lithium, beryllium and barium.
There's holmium and helium and hafnium and erbium,
And phosphorus and francium and fluorine and terbium,
And manganese and mercury, molybdenum, magnesium,
Dysprosium and scandium and cerium and caesium.
And lead, praseodymium, and platinum, plutonium,
Palladium, promethium, potassium, polonium,
And tantalum, technetium, titanium, tellurium,

[Pause for deep breath.]

And cadmium and calcium and chromium and curium.
There's sulphur, californium, and fermium, berkelium,
And also mendelevium, einsteinium, nobelium,

And argon, krypton, neon, radon, xenon, zinc and rhodium,

And chlorine, carbon, cobalt, copper, tungsten, tin and
sodium.

These are the only ones of which the news has come to
Ha'vard,

And there may be many others, but they haven't been
discavard!

In addition to the 102 listed above, a few more elements have since been discovered; namely, lawrencium, rutherfordium, dubnium, seaborgium, bohrium, hassium, meitnerium, darmstadtium, roentgenium, and seven others that have yet to be named.

Here are a few ways of remembering the first eighteen elements in the periodic table, which occupy the first three periods:

Periods 1–2 (Elements 1–10)

H	Hydrogen
He	Helium
Li	Lithium
Be	Beryllium
B	Boron
C	Carbon
N	Nitrogen
O	Oxygen
F	Fluorine
Ne	Neon

Happy Henry Likes Baking Big Cakes,
Not Omitting Floury Nuggets

Happy Henry Likes Beer
But Could Not Obtain Four Nuts

Period 3 (Elements 11–18)

Na	Sodium
Mg	Magnesium
Al	Aluminium
Si	Silicon
P	Phosphorus
S	Sulphur
Cl	Chlorine
Ar	Argon

Naughty Magpies Always Sing Perfect Songs
Clawing Ants

The Commonest Magnetic Material

The four commonest magnetic materials are Nickel,
Iron, Cobalt and Steel, which can be remembered by the
pithy saying:

Nick Irons Creased Shirts

Oxidation and Reduction

Oxidation is the loss of an electron by a molecule, atom or ion. Reduction is the opposite, i.e. the gain of an electron by molecule, atom or ion. A simple example of an oxidation–reduction reaction (you can't have one without the other) is the reaction of hydrogen gas with oxygen gas to form water: $2H_2 + O_2 = 2H_2O$

Many students have found the OILRIG acronym an invaluable method of understanding the process:

Oxidation **Is** **L**oss (of electrons)

Reduction **Is** **G**ain (of electrons)

Parts of an Atom

PEN is possibly the simplest acronym in the history of mnemonics:

Proton, **E**lectron, **N**eutron

CFCs

CFCs have invaded the language and the atmosphere. Chlorofluorocarbons were discovered in the 1920s by Thomas Midgley, an organic chemist at General Motors Corporation. They are a group of gases that are believed to contribute to global warming by eroding the ozone layer. The gases that come from leaking air conditioners, refrigerators and aerosols take ten to twenty years to reach the stratosphere and remain there for sixty-five years.

Because the word chlorofluorocarbons doesn't exactly trip off the tongue, some thoughtful soul had the idea of shortening the word to **CFC**, to keep this vital word in the forefront of our minds.

The Speed of Light

In the same way that it is possible to remember pi to different numbers of decimal places, a simple phrase also enables us to recall the speed of light in metres per second:

> We guarantee certainty, clearly referring to this light mnemonic = 299,792,458 m/sec.

Chemistry Experiments: A Warning

And here's a warning to all would-be chemists about the dangers of confusing water with sulphuric acid:

> Johnny was a chemist,
> But Johnny is no more,
> For what he thought was H_2O,
> Was H_2SO_4!

9
Britain:
A Brief History

———

Because there are so many dates and lists pertaining to emperors, kings, queens and presidents associated with world history, mnemonics have proved to be a perfect way of helping us to remember who did what to whom, where and when.

English Kings and Queens

It's a long roll call of names from William the Conqueror, and a long poem, but much more fun than just memorizing a list. For all its merits, though, it should be noted that the following verse misses out the nine-day reign of Lady Jane Grey in 1553 (in between the reigns of Edward VI and Mary I).

> Willie, Willie, Harry, Stee,
> Harry, Dick, John, Harry Three,
> One To Three Neds, Richard Two,
> Harrys Four Five Six . . . then who?

Edwards Four Five, Dick the Bad,
Harrys twain, Ned Six the lad,
Mary, Bessie, James you ken,
Then Charlie, Charlie, James again . . .

Will and Mary, Anne of gloria,
Georges Four!, Will Four, Victoria,
Edward Seven next, and then
Came George the Fifth in 1910.

Ned the Eight soon abdicated,
So George Six was coronated,
(or a George was reinstated)
Then number two Elizabeth.
And that's all folks, until her death . . .

(And for the probable future:
Charles Three and now I'm out of breath!)

(This poem is a traditional piece and naturally has been
extended over the years.)

For reference, this is the list of English kings and queens
in full, divided up according to the above verse:

William I 'the Conqueror' (1066–87), William II 'Rufus'
(1087–1100), Henry I (1100–35), Stephen (1135–54),
Henry II (1154–89), Richard I 'the Lionheart' (1189–99),
John (1199–1216), Henry III (1216–72), Edward I
(1272–1307), Edward II (1307–27), Edward III (1327–77),
Richard II (1377–1399), Henry IV (1399–1413),
Henry V (1413–22), Henry VI (1422–61, 1470–1)

Edward IV (1461–70, 1471–83), Edward V (1483),
Richard III (1483–5), Henry VII (1485–1509),
Henry VIII (1509–47), Edward VI (1547–53),
Mary I (1553–8), Elizabeth I (1558–1603), James I
(and VI of Scotland) (1603–25), Charles I (1625–49),
Charles II (1660–85), James II (and VII
of Scotland) (1685–8)

William III and Mary II (1689–94), William III
(1694–1702), Anne (1702–14), George I (1714–27),
George II (1727–60), George III (1760–1820),
George IV (1820–30), William IV (1830–7),
Victoria (1837–1901), Edward VII (1901–10),
George V (1910–36)

Edward VIII (1936), George VI (1936–52),
Elizabeth II (1952–).

British Monarchs and their Jubilees

The following simple phrase, used to represent the British monarchs who were on the throne for more than fifty years, worked perfectly until Queen Elizabeth II reached her Golden Jubilee in 2002 and overtook King Edward III in the list:

V and Three Thirds

The 'V' and the first three 'third' monarchs in question are:

Queen Victoria (1837–1901) – 64 years
King George III (1760–1820) – 60 years
King Henry III (1216–72) – 56 years
King Edward III (1327–77) – 51 years

The Six Wives of Henry VIII

Henry VIII (1491–1547) married six times in a quest to sire a son and heir. His decision to divorce his first wife and remarry was the root of the break with the Catholic Church in Rome and the dissolution of the monasteries.

m. 1510 – Catherine of Aragon (mother of Mary I)
m. 1533 – Anne Boleyn (mother of Elizabeth I)
m. 1536 – Jane Seymour (mother of Edward VI)
m. 1540 – Anne of Cleves
m. 1540 – Catherine Howard
m. 1543 – Catherine Parr

This is a rhythmic couplet used to remember their first names:

Kate 'n' Anne 'n' Jane, 'n' Anne 'n' Kate again 'n' again!

Using the initial letters of their surnames gives the phrase:

All Boys Should Come Home, Please

This memorable rhyme reveals the fate of Henry VIII's respective wives:

> Divorced, beheaded, died,
> Divorced, beheaded, survived.

British Royal Dynasties

From William the Conqueror to the current British monarch, there have been eight major royal houses since 1066:

Norman	(1066–1135)
Plantagenet	(1154–1399)
Lancaster	(1399–1461; 1470–1)
York	(1461–70, 1471–85)
Tudor	(1485–1603)
Stuart	(1603–49; 1660–1714)
Hanover	(1714–1901)
Windsor	(1901–to date)

As the **NPLYTSHW** list doesn't exactly trip off the tongue, these well-known phrases have been used as a more effective memory aid:

No **P**lan **L**ike **Y**ours **T**o **S**tudy **H**istory **W**isely

No **P**oint **L**etting **Y**our **T**rousers **S**lip **H**alf **W**ay

The Wars of the Roses

The battles between the Yorkists (white rose) and Lancastrians (red rose) were a series of intermittent civil wars fought over the English throne between 1455 and 1487. Although the white and red roses were emblems of each house, the 'Wars of the Roses' were not so called until the sixteenth century. The name derives from a scene in Shakespeare's *Henry VI Part 1* in which the two sides pick different coloured roses at the Temple Church in London.

St Albans (first battle, 1455)
Blore Heath (1459)
Northampton (1460)
Wakefield (1460)
Mortimer's Cross (1461)
St Albans (second battle, 1461)
Towton (1461)
Hedgeley Moor (1464)
Hexham (1464)
Barnet (1471)
Tewkesbury (1471)
Bosworth (1487)

To recall all the battles in chronological order, the phrase that follows has proved a useful saying for students of British history:

A Boy Now Will Mention
All The Hot Horrid Battles Till Bosworth

The Great Fire of London, 1666

To remember the year when the Great Fire of London ruined the medieval City of London from 2–5 September 1666, a pictorial mnemonic has often been used: think of the three sixes in 1666 resembling smoking chimneys on the skyline of the City of London.

Interestingly, when the year 1666 is set out in Roman numerals, it uses every letter once in descending order:

MDCLXVI

Marlborough's Victories

Here's how history scholars have been taught to remember the four important victories of John Churchill, first Duke of Marlborough, in the War of the Spanish Succession (1702–13). The battles in question are:

>**B**lenheim, 1704
>
>**R**amillies, 1706
>
>**O**uidenarde, 1708
>
>**M**alplaquet, 1709

Think of this code, **BROM 4689**, as an old-fashioned telephone number, using the initial capital letter of each battle location alongside the last digit of the year in which each battle was fought.

The disputes with France were ignited when King Charles II of Spain died without an heir. The Duke of Marlborough led a Grand Alliance comprising Britain, the Netherlands and Austria against the expanding French armies.

King George III (1760–1820)

The year that George III took the throne equals the number of yards in a mile, and from this coincidence a short verse was devised to aid maths and history scholars alike:

> George the Third said with a smile,
> 'Seventeen-sixty yards in a mile.'

Nelson's Injuries

During the Napoleonic Wars Nelson sustained numerous injuries. In 1794, at the Siege of Calvi, he lost the sight in his right eye when he was hit in the face by stone splinters after a cannonball hit a nearby building.

Three years later, during an attack on the Spanish base of Santa Cruz in the Canary Islands, Nelson's right arm was shattered by grapeshot and had to be amputated. So, to remember which parts of his anatomy Nelson lost in the course of duty, think EAR:

Eye, Arm – Right

10
World History

The Greek Philosophers

The names of the three most important Greek philosophers, in order of their dates of birth and also their influence, are:

Socrates (469–399 BC)
Plato (c.429–c.347 BC)
Aristotle (384–322 BC)

Socrates taught Plato and Plato taught Aristotle. Together they created the foundations of Western philosophy. Use your visual memory and imagine one or all of them meditating in a health **SPA**. Or think of the phrase: **S**mart **P**eople of **A**thens.

Roman Emperors

After Julius Caesar, the Roman general and statesman who became dictator of the Roman Empire before his assassination in 44 BC, the first five emperors of Rome were all Caesars. The first Emperor was Julius Caesar's adopted son (and great-nephew), Augustus, who handed down the title to his son-in-law Tiberius. From Augustus to Nero, Caesar's descendants, by adoption, marriage or birth, all inherited the family name:

Augustus	(31 BC–AD 14)
Tiberius	(AD 14–37)
Caligula	(AD 37–41)
Claudius	(AD 41–54)
Nero	(AD 54–68)

Here's a phrase to help remember the names by which they were most commonly known:

Another **T**om **C**at **C**aught **N**apping

The next six Roman emperors after Nero are **G**alba, **O**tho, **V**itellius, **V**espasian, **T**itus, **D**omitian:

At **T**he **C**at **C**lub **N**ever **G**ive **O**ut
Violent **V**ermin **T**o **D**ogs

The Seven Wonders of the World

The seven wonders of the ancient world were chronicled in the second century BC, but a list has been discovered in *The Histories* of Herodotus in the fifth century BC. The final list of amazing monuments to religion, mythology and art was compiled in the Middle Ages.

1. **S**tatue of Zeus at Olympia

2. **L**ighthouse (Pharos) of Alexandria

3. **M**ausoleum of Halicarnassus

4. **P**yramids of Egypt

5. **H**anging Gardens of Babylon

6. **T**emple of Artemis at Ephesus

7. **C**olossus of Rhodes

This mnemonic phrase has proved useful in remembering the seven wonders:

Seems **L**ike **M**ata **H**ari **P**icked **H**er **T**argets **C**arefully

Mythological Matters

Mnemosyne is the Greek goddess of memory, daughter of Gaia and Uranus. She lay with Zeus for nine nights and gave birth to the nine Muses: Calliope, Euterpe, Clio, Erato, Melpomene, Polyhymnia, Terpsichore, Thalia and Urania.

Carol Eats Crumpets,
Even More Plump Teas Than Usual

Carl Even Calls Eleven Men Plucky
Thomas Tank's Uncles

In classical art, the Muses are represented by emblems or mnemonic symbols, of which the masks of comedy and tragedy are probably the most familiar.

Name	Association	Mnemonic symbol
Calliope	chief of the muses and muse of epic poetry	writing tablet
Euterpe	muse of music	flute
Clio	muse of history	scroll and books
Erato	muse of love poetry	lyre and crown of roses
Melpomene	muse of tragedy	tragic mask
Polyhymnia	muse of sacred poetry	pensive expression
Terpsichore	muse of dance	dancing with a lyre
Thalia	muse of comedy	comic mask
Urania	muse of astronomy	staff and celestial globe

Joan of Arc

Also known as the Maid of Orléans, Joan of Arc (*c.*1412–31) was a French national heroine. She claimed that it was God's mission for her to reclaim her homeland from English domination towards the end of the Hundred Years War. She triumphed at the Siege of Orléans in 1429, which led to Charles VII's coronation at Reims, but was later captured at a skirmish near Compiègne. The English regent John of Lancaster, first Duke of Bedford, had her burned at the stake at Rouen aged only nineteen. She was canonized in 1920.

This mnemonic phrase describes the short career of Jeanne d'Arc:

ORLEANS CAMPAIGN RUIN

Orleans – victory – 1429

Compiègne – capture – 1430

Rouen – trial and death – 1431

Christopher Columbus Discovers America

The following verse was devised by American poet and former child prodigy Winifred Sackville Stoner Jr (1902–83). She was best known for writing mnemonic rhymes and poems to help people recall important information, particularly for educational purposes. One of her most famous poems is 'The History of the US', which starts with some lines on Christopher Columbus' discovery of the New World in 1492:

> In fourteen hundred, ninety-two,
> Columbus sailed the ocean blue.
> And found this land, land of the Free,
> beloved by you, beloved by me.

The Pilgrim Fathers

In 1620, the colonists of North America, known collectively as the Pilgrim Fathers, sailed in the *Mayflower* from Plymouth in England to America, landing at Cape Cod, Massachusetts.

The following short verse makes use of the twenty-four-hour clock to remind Americans when their forefathers first settled in the area:

> It's twenty past four,
> Let's go ashore.

US History in Brief

Other rhymes or phrases to recall aspects of American history include:

1776 – Signature of the American Declaration of Independence. The number of letters in each word in the following sentence stands for a numeral in the date:

'I sighted Thomas's rights.'

Winifred Sackville Stoner Jr's take on how we should remember the date of the Declaration of Independence goes like this:

> Year seventeen hundred seventy-six,
> July the fourth, this date please fix
> Within your minds, my children dear,
> for that was Independence Year.

And regarding the dark days of the American Civil War, she wrote:

> In eighteen hundred and sixty-one,
> an awful war was then begun
> Between the brothers of our land,
> who now together firmly stand.

Presidents of the USA

To date there have been forty-three US Presidents, which would make an incredibly long and complicated mnemonic phrase. The names of the first eleven Presidents are:

George **W**ashington (1789–97)
John **A**dams (1797–1801)
Thomas **J**efferson (1801–9)
James **M**adison (1809–17)
James **M**onroe (1817–25)
John Quincy **A**dams (1825–9)
Andrew **J**ackson (1829–37)
Martin van **B**uren (1837–41)
William Henry **H**arrison (1841)
John **T**yler (1841–5)
James **P**olk (1845–9)

Here's a question to ponder to help recall the first eleven:

Will **A J**olly **M**an **M**ake **A J**ust
But **H**arshly **T**reated **P**resident?

And if eleven is too many to remember, here's a phrase for the first seven:

Washington **A**nd **J**efferson **M**ade **M**any **A J**oke

The names of the middle American Presidents are:

Zachary **T**aylor (1849–50)
Millard **F**illmore (1850–3)

Franklin **P**ierce (1853–7)
James **B**uchanan (1857–61)
Abraham **L**incoln (1861–5)
Andrew **J**ohnson (1865–9)
Ulysses S. **G**rant (1869–77)
Rutherford B. **H**ayes (1877–81)
James **G**arfield (1881)
Chester **A**rthur (1881–5)
Grover **C**leveland (1885–9)
Benjamin **H**arrison (1889–93)
Grover **C**leveland (1893–7)
William **M**cKinley (1897–1901)

To recall this eminent list of fourteen, keep in mind the following phrase:

Taylor **F**elt **P**roud **B**ut **L**incoln **J**ust **G**rinned **H**appily, **G**argling, **A**nd **C**ould **H**ardly **C**ontain **M**cKinley

And finally, the Presidents of the twentieth century:

Theodore Roosevelt (1901–9)
William H. **T**aft (1909–13)
Woodrow **W**ilson (1913–21)
Warren **H**arding (1921–3)
Calvin **C**oolidge (1923–9)
Herbert **H**oover (1929–33)
Franklin D. Roosevelt (1933–45)
Harry S. **T**ruman (1945–53)
Dwight **E**isenhower (1953–61)

John F. Kennedy (1961–3)
Lyndon B. Johnson (1963–9)
Richard Nixon (1969–74)
Gerald Ford (1974–7)
Jimmy Carter (1977–81)
Ronald Reagan (1981–9)
George H. W. Bush (1989–93)
William J. Clinton (1992–2001)

Though it's quite a lengthy list, this saying might just make life easier:

Theodore Takes Wilson's Hand,
Cool Hoovering Franklin's True Experiences.
Ken, Justly Noted For Candour, Ruled But Coolly

The Heads on Mount Rushmore

Mount Rushmore is a world-famous national memorial in South Dakota that represents the first 150 years of American history with 60-foot-high granite carvings of the heads of four great US presidents: Washington, Jefferson, Lincoln and Roosevelt.

We Just Like Rushmore

11
Musical Interlude

———

Music can be a mnemonic device just by itself: many of us learned the alphabet to the well-known tune and rhythm of 'Twinkle, Twinkle, Little Star'. Similarly, advertisers use musical jingles to remind us of their products. For example, in just three descending notes composed by Johnny Johnson in 1967 we have: 'Beanz Meanz Heinz.' And who can forget the immortal line: 'Do the Shake'n'Vac and put the freshness back'?

Musical Notes

The first seven letters of the alphabet (A, B, C, D, E, F, G) are used in musical notation, which at least helps to keep things nice and simple. In the 1965 film *The Sound of Music*, Julie Andrews's character Maria makes the learning of music seem so easy.

Do–Re–Mi–Fa–So–La–Ti

Do = doe – a female deer
Re = ray – a drop of golden sun
Mi = me – a name I call myself
Fa = far – a long, long way to run

So = sew – a needle pulling thread
La = la – a note to follow 'so'
Ti = tea – a drink with jam and bread

Musical Staves

Learning to read music notation is almost impossible without the use of mnemonic tools. The musical stave is the set of five lines and four spaces on which notes indicate pitch and rhythm. The treble stave (or clef), indicating higher notes, is generally played with the right hand on the piano, and the bass stave (or clef), indicating lower notes, with the left hand.

Treble Clef: Lines

The notes on the lines of the treble clef are, from the lowest, E, G, B, D, F. They can be remembered with the following old chestnut:

Every **G**ood **B**oy **D**eserves **F**avour

Other variations include:

Every **G**lasgow **B**us **D**rives **F**ast

Every **G**ood **B**ird **D**oes **F**ly

Every **G**ood **B**oy **D**eserves **F**ruit

Treble Clef: Spaces

The notes on the spaces on the treble clef are, from the lowest, F, A, C, E. This pithy rhyme should help with learning the order of notes:

If the note's in a space, together they spell FACE.

Bass Clef: Lines

The order of notes on the lines of the bass clef are G, B, D, F, A. 'Good boys' feature once again in the catchy phrase devised to help musicians remember the basics:

Good **B**oys **D**eserve **F**ruit **A**lways

('Fruit' can, of course, be substituted for another more suitable f-word if necessary.)

Other variations include:

Good **B**oys **D**on't **F**ool **A**round

Great **B**ig **D**ogs **F**ight **A**lways

Good **B**ikes **D**on't **F**all **A**part

Great **B**ig **D**ucks **F**ly **A**way

Gentle **B**rown **D**onkeys **F**avour **A**pples

Bass Clef: Spaces

And thus it follows that the notes in the spaces of the bass clef are A, C, E, G. The following sayings act as a useful reminder of the four-note order:

All **C**ows **E**at **G**rass

All **C**ars **E**at **G**as

All **C**ats **E**at **G**oldfish

Musical Chord Progression

Music theory is not rocket science. There are twelve notes in Western music and all you need to do is add, subtract, multiply and divide. The notes – B, C, C$^\#$, D, D$^\#$, E, F, F$^\#$, G, G$^\#$, A, A$^\#$ – are all half a tone apart.

Major or minor chords are made up of the root note and the higher third and fifth notes, plus the seventh or eighth. The standard progression of chords is based on taking the fifth note as the root for the next chord. For example, in an F chord the fifth note is C, therefore the next chord is in the key of C, then G and so on: F, C, G, D, A, E, B:

Father **C**harles **G**oes **D**own **A**nd **E**nds **B**attle

Other variations include:

Father **C**hristmas **G**ets **D**runk **A**fter **E**very **B**eer

Fat **C**ats **G**o **D**eaf **A**fter **E**ating **B**ats

Five **C**ool **G**uys **D**anced **A**way **E**very **B**eat

And in reverse for the flat keys the mnemonic can be reversed: B, E, A, D, G, C, F:

Battle **E**nds **A**nd **D**own **G**oes **C**harles's **F**ather

Bottles **E**mpty **A**nd **D**own **G**oes **C**harles's **F**ather

Be **E**xciting **A**nd **D**aring, **G**o **C**limb **F**ences

Choral Voices

There are four different voice ranges that one can hear in a quartet whose initial letters helpfully spell out STAB:

Soprano
Tenor
Alto
Bass

Musical Modes or Scales

The modes as based on the white piano keys beginning at C are:

Ionian mode – the familiar major scale in which most popular music is written.

Dorian mode – most often heard in Celtic music, with a melancholy feel.

Phrygian mode – used especially by guitar soloists in counterpoint to an Ionian mode.

Lydian mode – popular in jazz music, with a mix of major and minor chord progressions.

Mixolydian mode – major feel with minor intervals and popular with soloists as a counterpoint to an Ionian mode.

Aeolian mode – in a minor key and produces a sense of sadness.

Locrian mode – the intervals are considered unsatisfactory and most composers find it unworkable.

Named after Greek cities that are thought to reflect the moods of the seven modes, one way of remembering the order of the modes is to recall this phrase:

I Don't **P**lay **L**ike **M**y **A**unt **L**ucy

12
Foreign Tongues

French Plurals with an X

Here's a verse to tell you which French nouns require the letter 'x' rather than 's', when they are used in the plural:

> *Bijou, caillou, chou,*
> *Genou, hibou, joujou . . .*
> *Pou!*

The English translation of the verse is:

> Jewel, pebble, cabbage,
> Knee, owl, toy . . .
> Flea!

Or commit this rhyme to memory:

> *Mes choux, mes bijoux,*
> *Lassez vous joujoux,*
> *Venez sur mes genoux!*
> *Regardez ces mauvais petits garçons,*
> *Qui jettent des cailloux a ces pauvres hiboux!*

Counting to Six in French

The correct words for one to six in French are *un, deux, trois, quatre, cinq* and *six*. Try to picture this dark story of how to control the cat population:

> *Un, deux, trois,* cat sank – cease, please!

French Verbs Using *Être*

All French verbs that use *être* in the perfect tense rather than *avoir* indicate a particular kind of movement. The thirteen main verbs (and four derivatives) can be recalled using the popular mnemonic phrase **Dr & Mrs P Vandertramp**:

Devenir **R**evenir & **M**onter **R**ester **S**ortir
Passer **V**enir **A**ller **N**aître **D**escendre **E**ntrer
Rentrer **T**omber **R**etourner **A**rriver
Mourir **P**artir

Alternatively, the acronym ADVENT is another useful way to recall the main *être* verbs. Each letter stands for one of the verbs and its opposite, with the thirteenth verb *retourner* standing alone.

Arriver – Partir
Descendre – Monter
Venir – Aller
Entrer – Sortir
Naître – Mourir
Tomber – Rester
Retourner

Japanese Vowels

The pronunciation and lexical ordering of the Japanese vowels is AIUEO. Using this short phrase you can understand the exact pronunciation of the vowels:

Ah we soon get old

Counting to Ten in Japanese

Numeral	Japanese word	Sounds like
1	Ichi	Itchy
2	Ni	Knee
3	San	Sun
4	Shi	She
5	Go	Go
6	Roko	Rocko
7	Shichi	Shi Shi
8	Hachi	Hatchy
9	Kyu	Queue
10	Ju	Jew

Days of the Week in French, Spanish and Italian

The seven-day week has been with us for almost 2,000 years. The Romans allocated one of the seven planets to each of the days of the week: the sun, moon and the five planets that shine brightly in the night sky – Mars, Mercury, Jupiter, Venus and Saturn.

	Planet	French	Spanish	Italian
Sunday	Sun	Dimanche	Domingo	Domenica
Monday	Moon	Lundi	Lunes	Lunedì
Tuesday	Mars	Mardi	Martes	Martedì

	Planet	**French**	**Spanish**	**Italian**
Wednesday	Mercury	Mercredi	Miércoles	Mercoledì
Thursday	Jupiter	Jeudi	Jueves	Giovedì
Friday	Venus	Vendredi	Viernes	Venerdì
Saturday	Saturn	Samedi	Sábado	Sabato

By recalling the planets after which the days were named, it helps to jog the memory when remembering the days of the week in the Latin-based languages.

This traditional rhyme is derived from some of the characteristics of the planets:

> Monday's child is fair of face,
> Tuesday's child is full of grace,
> Wednesday's child is full of woe,
> Thursday's child has far to go;
> Friday's child is loving and giving,
> Saturday's child works hard for a living,
> But the child that is born on the Sabbath day
> Is bonny and blithe, good and gay.

The Greek Alphabet

For those wishing to learn the Greek alphabet, you can memorize the order of the twenty-four letters by singing along to the tune of 'Twinkle, Twinkle, Little Star', but if you're no longer a child it might be better not to practise out loud . . .

Alpha, Beta, Gamma, Delta,
Epsilon, Zeta, Eta, Theta,
Iota, Kappa, Lambda, Mu,
Nu, Xi, Omicron, Pi,
Rho, Sigma, Tau, Upsilon,
Phi, Chi, Psi kai Omega.

NB: Ϗ (kai) means 'and' in Greek.

The Runic Alphabet

The Runic alphabet is also known as FUTHARK, after the first six letters in the alphabet – namely *f, u, th, a, r,* and *k.* Runes were used by Scandinavians and Anglo-Saxons around the third century. There are twenty-four letters comprising eighteen consonants and six vowels.

The Runic characters are a series of glyphs that represent sounds and ideas, based on the hieroglyphs of Ancient Egypt. They were not only used to convey sacred meaning, but also mysteries and secrets. It is not known why the letters were ordered in this way, but the word FUTHARK is thought to be an ancient mnemonic.

13
Religious Matters

For Christians, most of the religious tuition we received as children would have been at Sunday school or in religious-education classes. As well as listening to countless Bible stories, there were also many rhymes and sayings we were taught that simplified certain matters of religion, which helped keep the vast subjects of the Old and New Testaments more clearly in mind.

The Twelve Apostles

The twelve chief followers of Jesus are recalled in a well-known Sunday-school rhyme:

> This is the way the disciples run
> Peter, Andrew, James and John
> Philip and Bartholomew
> Thomas next and Matthew, too.
> James the less and Judas the greater
> Simon the zealot and Judas the traitor.

An alternative shorter method uses the following line:

> Bart And John Fill (Phil) Tom's Matt with 2 Jameses,
> 2 Simons* and 2 Judases.

> *Peter was originally Simon or Simon-Peter,
> hence there are two Simons in the second verse.

The Four Gospels

With regard to the first four books of the New Testament (the Gospels), various rhymes have been devised to help children to remember them (and their order) more easily.

> Matthew, Mark, Luke and John
> Went to bed with their trousers on.

The above verse is probably derived from the following traditional poem, of which there are two versions:

Matthew, Mark, Luke and John
Bless the bed that I lie on;
Before I lay me down to sleep,
I give my soul to Christ to keep.

Matthew, Mark, Luke and John
Bless the bed that I lie on;
Four corners to my bed,
Four angels round my head;
One to watch, one to pray,
And two to bear my soul away!

The Ten Commandments

The Ten Commandments are a list of rules for living a good and moral life. According to the Old Testament they are the word of God, inscribed on two stone tablets and given to Moses on Mount Sinai. James Muirden, author of *The Rhyming Bible*, has cleverly summed them up in an unforgettable verse comprising six rhyming couplets:

The First Law set by God in stone
reads *Worship me, and me alone!*
The next says Idols are profane;
the Third, don't take my Name in vain;
the Fourth says keep the Seventh Day free;
the Fifth, treat Parents properly;

the Sixth says Murdering is wrong
(you knew the Seventh all along*);
the Eighth is crystal clear on Thieving,
as is the Ninth, on Not Deceiving;
and now the last of all His laws –
don't Covet things that are not yours.

*The Seventh, of course, forbids adultery.

We can also remind ourselves of the commandments with this cheeky sentence:

One idle damn Sunday, Dad killed cheating thief
and lied to cover it.

i.e. one God; no idols; don't swear; keep the Sabbath; honour your father (and mother); don't kill; don't commit adultery; don't steal; don't bear false witness; don't covet.

Books of the Old Testament

Although there are a total of thirty-nine books in the Old Testament, this memorable verse has made it much easier to remember them all in order:

That great Jehovah speaks to us,
In Genesis and Exodus,
Leviticus and Numbers see,
Followed by Deuteronomy,

Joshua and Judges sway the land,
Ruth gleans a sheaf with trembling hand;
Samuel and numerous Kings appear,
Whose Chronicles we wondering hear.
Ezra and Nehemiah now,
Esther, the beauteous mourner show.
Job speaks in sighs, David in Psalms,
The Proverbs teach to scatter alms.
Ecclesiastes then come on,
And the sweet Song of Solomon.
Isaiah, Jeremiah then,
With Lamentations takes his pen,
Ezekiel, Daniel, Hosea's lyres,
Swell Joel, Amos, Obadiah's.
Next Jonah, Micah, Nahum come,
And lofty Habakkuk finds room.
While Zephaniah, Haggai calls,
Rapt Zechariah builds his walls,
And Malachi, with garments rent,
Concludes the Ancient Testament.

The Ten Biblical Plagues of Egypt

From Exodus 7:14–12:36, these are the ten catastrophes
that God inflicted upon Egypt:

River to blood
Frogs
Lice
Flies
Murrain (disease)
Boils
Hail
Locusts
Darkness
Firstborn

If the list proves too tricky to remember, the following sentence is a memorable means of recalling the order and initial letter of each plague:

Retreating **F**rom **L**ong **F**light **M**cDonald
Battered **H**ostile **L**eader **D**emanding **F**ries

The Seven Deadly Sins

We have seven days of the week, seven colours in the rainbow, seven wonders of the world, and for those who have not taken their Bible studies to heart, we have seven deadly sins:

Anger, **P**ride, **C**ovetousness, **L**ust, **S**loth, **E**nvy, **G**reed

To help make the list of sins easier to memorize, some God-fearing person devised the following mnemonic phrase:

All **P**rivate **C**olleges **L**eave **S**erious **E**ducational **G**aps

Or to put it another way:

Pride, **E**nvy, **W**rath, **S**loth, **A**varice, **G**luttony, **L**ust
PEWS 'Ave GLu

The Ten States of Mind

In the Buddhist construct, there are ten states of mind:

1. **H**ell, the state of suffering
2. **H**unger, the state of base needs
3. **A**nimalism, the state of beastly power
4. **A**nger, the state of loathing
5. **N**eutrality, the state of neither one thing nor another
6. **R**apture, the state of joy
7. **L**earning, the state of being mentally open
8. **R**ealization, the state of receiving/living wisdom
9. **B**odhisattva, the state of compassion
10. **B**uddha, the state of perfection

All of which mental agony and ecstasy gives us:

Has **H**annah **A**rranged **A**ll **N**ovices **R**unning **L**ate, **R**equired **B**efore **B**uddha?

14

The Human Body

Young medics are faced with masses of dull and lengthy lists of complicated words that represent the workings of the human body. Without a wide range of useful and often amusing memory aids, it would be impossible for them to remember everything.

The Vital Processes of Life

Collectively, these are known as **MRS GREN**:

Movement, **R**espiration, **S**ensitivity,
Growth, **R**eproduction, **E**xcretion, **N**utrition

The Human Brain

The brain is the most complex structure at the nub of all human decisions, communications and activities. The cerebral cortex is divided into four sections or lobes:

Frontal, **P**arietal, **O**ccipital, **T**emporal

First **P**lace **O**ften **T**rounces

Cranial Bones

Occipital, Parietal, Frontal, Temporal,
Ethmoid, Sphenoid

Old People From Texas Eat Spiders

Cranial Nerves

How many med students learned the twelve cranial nerves sung to the tune of 'The Twelve Days of Christmas'?
    The first and second verses start off:

I (Olfactory)
On the first nerve of the cranium,
my true love gave to me:
My sense olfactory.

II (Optic)
On the second nerve of the cranium,
my true love gave to me:
Two eyes a-looking,
And my sense olfactory.

The song gets quite lengthy, so the final verse is:

XII (Hypoglossal)
On the twelfth nerve of the cranium,
my true love gave to me:
Twelve lovely lickings, (Hypoglossal)
Eleven heads a-tilting, (Spinal accessory)

Ten heartbeats a minute, (Vagus)
Nine quick swallows, (Glossopharyngeal)
Eight sounds, and balance, (Auditory)
Seven funny faces, (Facial)
Six sideways glances, (Abducens)
Mas-ti-ca-tion! (Trigeminal)
Four superior oblique muscles, (Trochlear)
Three cross-eyed glances, (Oculomotor)
Two eyes a-looking, (Optic)
And my sense olfactory. (Olfactory)

In addition to the song, there is also a catchy phrase to recall when remembering the names of the cranial nerves:

On **O**ld **O**lympus's **T**owering **T**op,
A Fat-**A**rsed **G**erman **V**iewed **S**ome **H**ops

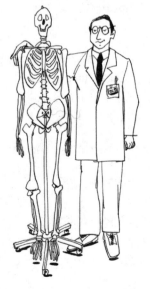

Bones of the Human Body

BONES OF THE UPPER LIMB OR ARM:
Scapula, Clavicle, Humerus, Ulna, Radius, Carpals,
Metacarpals, Phalanges

Some Crooks Have Underestimated Royal Canadian
Mounted Police

BONES OF THE LOWER LIMB OR LEG:
Hip, Femur, Patella, Tibia, Fibula, Tarsals,
Metatarsals, Phalanges

Help Five Police To Find Ten Missing Prisoners

BONES OF THE WRIST (CARPAL):
Scaphoid, Lunate, Triquetrum, Pisiform, Trapezium,
Trapezoid, Capitate, Hamate

Some Lovers Try Positions That They Can't Handle

VERTEBRAE OR BONES OF THE SPINAL COLUMN
(SUPERIOR TO INFERIOR):
Cervical, Dorsal,* Lumbar, Sacrum, Coccyx

Clever Dick Looks Silly Clot!

Canned Tuna Looks So Cramped

* Dorsal vertebrae are also known as Thoracic,
hence the alternative phrase.

SHOULDER MUSCLES OR ROTATOR CUFF
Teres minor, Infraspinatus, Supraspinatus, Subscapular

Tarts In Silk Stockings

Bone Fracture Types

Once medical students have learned the names of the bones, they can use the **GO C3PO** acronym to learn the ways in which the bones can get broken.

Greenstick, **O**pen, **C**omplete/**C**losed/**C**omminuted, **P**artial, **O**thers

Skin Layers

Mnemonic sentences help medics to remember the order of skin layers or nerves so that when they become surgeons and start brandishing scalpels, they can identify which bit to cut through first. They use the aptly named **SCALP** acronym:

Skin, **C**onnective tissue, **A**poneurosis, **L**oose areolar tissue, **P**eriosteum

Excretion

For the excretory organs of the body, think **SKILL**:

Skin, **K**idneys, **I**ntestines, **L**iver, **L**ungs

The Properties of Bile

Here's a catchy ditty to keep the properties of bile in mind:

Bile from the liver emulsifies greases
Tinges the urine and colours the faeces
Aids peristalsis, prevents putrefaction
If you remember all this you'll give satisfaction.

For doctors dealing with patients who are possible suicide risks, the **SAD PERSONS** checklist always come in handy:

Sex (male or female)

Age (old or young)

Depression

Previous suicide attempts

Ethanol and other drugs

Reality testing/**R**ational thought (loss of)

Social support lacking

Organized suicide plan

No spouse

Sickness/**S**tated future intent

Signs of Mania

Medics have to **DIG FAST** to identify key symptoms of manic behaviour:

Distractibility
Indiscretion ('excessive involvement
in pleasurable activities')
Grandiosity
Flight of ideas
Activity increase
Sleep deficit (decreased need for sleep)
Talkativeness (pressured speech)

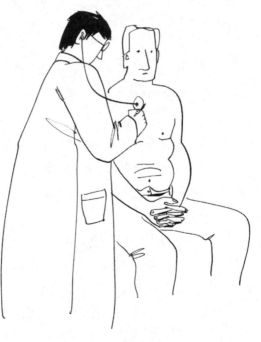

Signs of Schizophrenia

If doctors suspect a patient may have schizophrenia, they will check for **WHID**:

Withdrawn, **H**allucinations
Inappropriate emotional response, **D**elusions

Signs of Anxiety Disorder

Your GP will test for **MR FISC** if you're suffering from GAD – General Anxiety Disorder:

Motor tension
Restlessness
Fatigue
Irritability
Sleep disturbances
Concentration difficulty

The Heart

The signs of heart failure are ABCDE:

Acidosis, **B**lue skin, **C**old skin, **D**ilated heart,
Edema (oedema in the UK)

Hangover Signs

You know you've a hangover when you feel like **SHIT**:

Shakes/**S**eizures/**S**weats/**S**tomach pains
Hallucinosis (auditory)
Increased vitals/**I**nsomnia
Tremens (delirium tremens – the lethal part)

Fever Facts

Your doctor will check the **FACTS** to diagnose influenza
or just 'man flu', i.e. a cold:

Fever
Aches
Chills
Tiredness
Sudden symptoms

Vitamins Are Good For You

We all need vitamins to maintain a good level of health.
This rhyme reminds us of the important qualities of each
and every vitamin:

Vitamin A keeps the cold germs away
And tends to make meek people nervy,
B's what you need
When you're going to seed,
And C is specific in scurvy.
Vitamin D makes the bones in your knee
Tough and hard for the service on Sunday,
While E makes hens scratch
And increases the hatch
And brings in more profits on Monday.
Vitamin F never bothers the chef
For this vitamin never existed.
G puts the fight in the old appetite
And you eat all the foods that are listed.
So now when you dine remember these lines;
If long on this globe you will tarry.
Just try to be good and pick out more food
From the orchard, the garden and dairy.

Doctors' Shorthand

Doctors-to-be develop their sense of humour as students and refine it throughout their careers. Consequently, doctors have been known to write F BUNDY on patients' notes if the prognosis is grim:

F*ed But Unfortunately Not Dead Yet**

15
Life-Saving Tips

Reminding yourself of how to save a life might be the best thing you ever do, so pay attention and refresh your memory of the many first-aid-related acronyms in existence.

The main aim of First Aid is the **3 Ps**:

Preserve life
Prevent deterioration in the patient's condition
Promote recovery

ABC is the traditional and essential way to remember what to check when administering cardiopulmonary resuscitation on a casualty:

Airways

Breathing

Circulation

Here are two lots of **3 Bs** to remember when dealing with an accident victim:

Check **B**reath **B**efore **B**lood (flow)
And then **B**lood **B**efore **B**ones

Keep calm in an emergency and think **AMEGA**:

Assess the situation
Make the area safe
Emergency aid
Get help
Aftermath

How alert is your casualty? Check for **AVPU**:

Alert
Voice
Pain
Unconscious

Is the casualty in circulatory shock? Look for **PCFATS**:

Pale
Cold and **C**lammy skin
Fast pulse
Anxious
Thirsty
Sick

Assess the injuries. Look at areas of soft tissue and bones and think **RICE**:

Rest
Ice/**I**mmobilize
Compression
Elevation

If your casualty is lucid, ask these **AMPLE** questions:

Allergies – do they have any?
Medication – are they taking any?
Past history – do they have any prior medical problems?
Last meal – what/when did they last eat?
Environment – do they know where they are?

If the injured party is in a coma, it could be caused by any of the following **MIDAS** problems:

Meningitis
Intoxication
Diabetes
Air (respiratory failure)
Subdural/**S**ubarachnoid haemorrhage

Or by **COMA**:

CO$_2$ (carbon dioxide) and **C**O (carbon monoxide) excess
Overdose: drugs such as insulin, paracetamol, etc.
Metabolic: BSL (blood sugar level), Na+ (sodium), K+ (potassium), Mg^2+ (magnesium), urea, ammonia, etc.
Apoplexy: stroke, meningitis, encephalitis, cerebral abscess, etc.

Keep the word **FAST** in mind when assessing the condition of a possible stroke victim:

Face: is one side of the face drooping downwards?
Arm: can the person raise both arms?
Speech: is the person's speech slurred or confusing;
is the person unable to speak?
Time: time is critical.
Call an ambulance immediately.

If you witness a person collapsing, what could have caused it? Think **I'VE FALLEN**:

Illness
Vestibular (balance problem)
Environmental
Feet or **F**ootwear
Alcohol and/or drugs
Low blood pressure
Low oxygen status
Ears or **E**yes
Neuropathy

Is the patient in shock? If so, he/she might be suffering from any one of the **Royal Navy CHAMPS** range of shocks:

Respiratory
Neurogenic
Cardiogenic
Haemorrhagic
Anaphylactic
Metabolic
Psychogenic
Septic

Survival Techniques

If it's a case of personal survival out in the wilds, use extreme survival expert Ray Mears's word **STOP**:

Stop
Take inventory
Orientate
Plan

Mr Mears also has a useful way for reminding himself of a checklist for his vehicle before setting out on a journey, using the acronym **PETROL**:

Petrol, **E**lectrolyte (i.e. battery), **T**yres,
Radiator, **O**il, **L**ights

In the event of discovering a fire, think **FIRE**.

Find the fire
Inform people by shouting out
Restrict the spread of fire (if it is safe to do so)
Evacuate the area/**Ex**tinguish the fire
(if it is safe to do so)

Driving a Car

Mirror **S**ignal **M**anoeuvre is an essential phrase drummed into all learner drivers, but it's one that drivers should never forget. Say it to yourself before you start, turn, change lane, reverse and stop. It's a motorist's way of applying the 'Look Before You Leap' principle.

Don't forget to belt up too:

'Clunk Click, Every Trip.'

Road Safety

When learning to cross the road, British children of all ages have been strongly advised to remember these life-saving lines:

Look Right, Look Left, Then Right Again
Stop, Look and Listen

The Green Cross Code campaign was launched in the mid-1970s, and the 'Green Cross' character was played by David Prowse, of Darth Vader fame. His memorable slogan was: 'I won't be there when you cross the road / So always use the Green Cross Code.'

Doctor Who actor Jon Pertwee also had a Green Cross Code role in a 1976 public information film, in which he gave us the quirky mnemonic SPLINK, which stood for:

Find a **S**afe place to cross
Stand on the **P**avement
Look for traffic
If traffic is coming, let it pass
When there is **N**o traffic near, walk across the road
Keep looking and listening for traffic as you cross

The campaign continues today with the help of animated hedgehogs helping kids to remember this simplified six-part list:

1. Think first
2. Stop
3. Use your eyes and ears
4. Wait until it's safe to cross
5. Look and listen
6. Arrive alive

16
The World of Work

The world of business and employment can be a cut-throat one, which is why it helps to be ahead of the game and gain an advantage over competitors whether they be individuals or entire companies.

Business Internet Domain Names

As with all aspects of selling yourself, choosing a name for your website is as vital as any other way of making sure people notice your business and, most importantly, remember it.

Here's the list that the UK Freeserve website define as the key to success: **RAIL**

Recall	Will the name be easy to remember?
Aesthetics	How will the name look on the screen or on paper?
Impressions	First impressions always count.
Length	Keep it short and sweet. Less is definitely more.

Business Presentations

In any type of public meeting, seminar or lecture, never forget your **ABC** and always be:

Accurate, Brief and Clear

PPPPP

To give a good presentation, plan ahead and remember the **5 Ps**:

Proper Planning Prevents Poor Performance

PRIDE

Whatever line of work you're in – take **PRIDE** in what you're doing:

Personal Responsibility In Daily Efforts

To B or not to B

Be Brave and Believe; and don't be Boring or Bashful.

KISS

No matter how you earn a living, never forget to:

Keep **I**t **S**imple, **S**tupid

The **KISS** acronym is applied from principles of business, advertising, computer operating systems to science and learning. Albert Einstein's maxim was: 'Everything should be made as simple as possible, but no simpler.'

SWOT Analysis

SWOT is a study of four crucial elements of a business's planning process:

Strengths, **W**eaknesses, **O**pportunities, **T**hreats

Never ASSUME Anything

Every business person knows that assumption is the mother of all screw-ups:

To assume makes an **ASS** out of **U** and **ME**.

Office Egos

In the world of employment and life in general it's sometimes wise to keep your ego under control to avoid making enemies of at least half the population. Stick to the **FASTA** technique:

Focus on your goals, not just on yourself.
Ask for other people's opinions.
    You can learn from others.
Say thank you. Always a good idea in any situation.
Treat everyone as your equal.
    Other people know stuff that you don't.
Allow yourself to fail.
    We learn from our mistakes.

Sales Techniques

If you have something to sell, always **PLAN** in advance:

Prepare with research (don't forget your 5 Ps)
Lose time, lose all
Analyse the situation
Never just call (always have a good reason
    to make contact if you are making a 'cold call')

During a sales pitch, meeting or presentation, these should be your **AIMS**:

> **A**rrest the senses
> **I**nterest by questions and novelty
> **M**ove by proof and demonstration
> **S**ucceed in getting a 'yes'

Think **ETC** after the pitch has been made:

> **E**valuate the outcome
> **T**each yourself and others
> **C**heck for results

How to Interview

The first mnemonic a journalist learns is the five Ws and the H. The worst moment during an interview is when the subject gives only yes or no answers. Phrasing a question with these words gets people talking and should prevent single-word replies.

Who? When? Where? What? Why? How?

SMART

This mnemonic is used for setting goals and it's a powerful tool for personal planning and kickstarting your career. Setting goals is all about knowing what you want to achieve and where to concentrate your efforts. You have to be **SMART**! Your daily 'to do' list must be:

Specific, **M**easurable, **A**ttainable, **R**elevant, **T**ime bound

AIDA

Advertisers need people to remember which products to buy and so they design arresting images and messages for us consumers. The key principles of advertising are:

Attract **A**ttention – 'Look at that!'
Arouse **I**nterest – 'Mmm, that looks interesting!'
Create **D**esire – 'I want it!'
Urge **A**ction – 'Now!'

Job Interview Techniques

Preparation for meetings is vital in business and job interviews are possibly the most important meetings in business life. Your aim at an interview is to sell yourself – you are the product. Hence the need for the **STAR** system:

Situation – Describe your previous experience of situations that you have managed successfully.
TAsk – Give details of exactly how you managed the situation. What was your contribution to the task? A tip from the professionals – don't make it up and don't exaggerate because you'll be found out!
Result – Congratulations. You're hired!

17
A Miscellany
of Mnemonics

Champagne Bottles

Name	Capacity	No. of Bottles
Quarter	18.75 cl	–
Half-bottle	37.5 cl	–
Bottle	75 cl	1
Magnum	1.5 l	2
Jeroboam	3 l	4
Rehoboam	4.5 l	6
Methuselah	6 l	8
Salmanazar	9 l	12
Balthazar	12 l	16
Nebuchadnezzar	15 l	20

One way to recall the names of differently sized bottles of champagne is to think of a detective in the company of some ancient men:

Magnum – 1980s TV private detective
(or ice cream or gun)

Jeroboam – Founder and first King of Israel,
931–910 BC
Rehoboam – Son of Solomon, King of Judah,
922–908 BC
Methuselah – Biblical patriarch who lived
to the age of 969
Salmanazar – King of Assyria, 859–824 BC
Balthazar – Son of Nabonide, Regent of Babylon, 539 BC
Nebuchadnezzar – King of Babylon, 605–562 BC

Otherwise this rude mnemonic could jog your memory:

My Joanna Really Makes Splendid Burping Noises

Alcohol Tips

Few people need tips on drinking alcohol, but some
drinkers swear by the advice offered in this rhyme:

> Beer on whisky? Very risky!
> Whisky on beer, never fear . . .

We all know that mixing drinks isn't a wise thing to do, but
the warning quote below says it succinctly and honestly:

> Never mix grape with the grain.

Steering a Boat

If you find yourself behind the wheel of a boat, it helps to
recall which side of the boat is port (the left side with red
lights) and starboard (the right side with green lights).
Fortunately, there are several ways to jog one's memory:

> PORT has four letters and so has LEFT
>
> P (port) comes before S (starboard) in the alphabet,
> as L (left) comes before R (right)
>
> PORT wine should be LEFT alone when it is RED
> (therefore starboard is RIGHT)
>
> PORT is a RED wine,
> and RED is the LEFT side of politics
>
> There's a little RED PORT LEFT in the bottle

Five Sailing Essentials

This handy phrase reminds the crew of a boat of the 'Five Essentials' of sailing:

Can The Boat Sail Correctly?

Course to steer – the course might be a particular bearing (as, say, 250 degrees) or at a particular angle to the apparent wind.

Trim – the fore and aft balance of the boat. The moveable ballast on the boat is of course the crew, and the aim is to achieve an even keel.

Balance – the port and starboard balance. This is also about adjusting the weight inboard or outboard.

Sail – this is to ensure the sails are set correctly until they fill with wind. The front edge or luff of the sail should be in line with the wind.

Centreboard – if the boat has a moveable centreboard, it should be lowered when sailing close to the wind. It is raised on a downwind course to reduce drag.

Left and Right

An oft-heard criticism of some organizations is that the right hand doesn't know what the left hand is doing, which is a bit of a problem if you can't even tell the difference.

A quick physical mnemonic you can use to remember is to place your left hand palm down, rotate your left thumb 90°clockwise, so that the forefinger and thumb makes the shape of L for Left.

Interest Rates

Every city slicker knows this one:

> When rates are low
> Stocks will grow.
> When rates are high
> Stocks will die.

A Game of Bridge

The Order of Suits from highest to lowest are:

Spades, **H**earts, **D**iamonds, **C**lubs

If the order of suits just won't stick in your mind, try remembering the following fact:

Sally **H**as **D**irty **C**hildren

Basic DIY Techniques

So you've found the screwdriver, climbed the ladder, but you don't know which way to turn the screw because it was secured so tightly the last time round? This invaluable expression will guarantee that you don't waste precious minutes trying to unscrew a screw the wrong way:

> Righty-tighty,
> Lefty-loosey.

Or how about:

> Right on; left off.

British Hereditary Titles

According to *Burke's Peerage*, there are five grades of the peerage which can only be inherited by the eldest son or given by the state:

Duke, **M**arquis, **E**arl, **V**iscount, **B**aron

This short list can also be remembered using the following phrases:

Does **M**ilord **E**ver **V**isit **B**righton?

Did **M**ary **E**ver **V**isit **B**ognor?

Correct Forms of Address

Here's a short verse to remind us how to address people with letters after their name:

> Honour before degree,
> Degree before MP.

Therefore the old soldier's name should be written as:

> Mr J. Smith, VC, MA

And the Member of Parliament's will be:

> John Smith Esq, OBE, BSc, MP.

Faithfully or Sincerely?

The correct way to sign off a letter is to use 'Yours sincerely' if you know the recipient's name, and have addressed the letter directly to him or her, and to use 'Yours faithfully' if you are sending it to an unknown person, and have begun the letter 'Dear Sir'.

As it can be tricky to recall when to use which sign-off with which mode of address, the simplest way to remember is to keep in mind the rule: **Never Two Ss Together**. Thus a letter addressed 'Dear **S**ir' should never end 'Yours **s**incerely'.

The Great Outdoors

If you're invited on a huntin', shootin' and fishin' weekend with the boss, remember the following acronym: **BRASS**.

Breathe, **R**elax, **A**im, **S**ight, **S**queeze

By keeping this sequence in mind, it might help you to shoot a rifle without missing your targets by a mile, or at least make you seem as if you know what you're doing . . .

Select Bibliography

Chambers School Spelling (Chambers Harrap, 2003)

Demonic Mnemonics, Murray Suid (Frank Schaffer Publications, Inc., 1981)

A Dictionary of Mnemonics (Eyre Methuen, 1972)

Fowler's Modern English Usage, R. W. Burchfield (OUP, 2004)

How To Develop A Brilliant Memory Week By Week, Dominic O'Brien (Duncan Baird Publishers, 2005)

Medico Mnemonica, E. S. Marlowe MD (PMIC, 1997)

The Memory Doctor, Douglas J. Mason and Spencer Xavier Smith (New Harbinger Publications, Inc., 2005)

Your Memory: How It Works And How To Improve It, Kenneth L. Higbee Ph.D. (Prentice-Hall, Inc., 1977)

If you enjoyed this book, look out for:

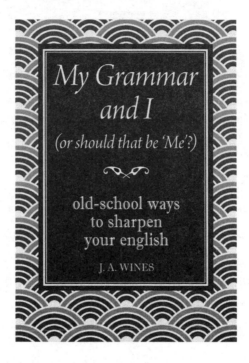

My Grammar and I
and I

(or should that be 'Me'?)

old-school ways
to sharpen
your english

J. A. WINES

Published: October 2008

Price: £9.99

ISBN: 978-1-84317-310-6